Y0-BZN-135

THE SHAKESPEARE PARALLEL TEXT SERIES

A MIDSUMMER NIGHT'S DREAM

Edited by
Janie B. Yates-Glandorf, Ph.D.

Cover illustration by
Heather Cooper

PERFECTION LEARNING CORPORATION
Logan, Iowa

1000 North Second Avenue
Logan, Iowa 51546

Printed in the U.S.A.

The Past is Prologue

Shakespeare lives! So writes his most eminent biographer, S. Schoenbaum, in the prologue to *Shakespeare: The Globe and the World* (New York: Oxford University Press, 1979). And the evidence is all around us.

We find it in the language we use. When we lament that "the course of true love never did run smooth," whether we are conscious of it or not, we are quoting from *A Midsummer Night's Dream*. When we observe that a well-intended law or regulation is "more honor'd in the breach than the observance," we are applying — or perhaps misapplying — a phrase from *Hamlet*. When we inscribe "What's past is prologue" on the National Archives building in our nation's capital, we are dignifying a minor line from *The Tempest*. Often without realizing it, we find ourselves speaking, if only momentarily, in the accents of a Portia or a Polonius, a Macbeth or a Mercutio. And when we *do* realize it — when we are conscious of the Shakespearean idiom embedded in so much of our daily speech — we take pleasure in those subtle turns of phrase that continue to enrich our discourse. A veteran gardener recently observed, for example, that anyone who calls a rose by any other name has probably been pruning.

Alongside the Greek classics and the King James version of the Bible, Shakespeare's words and works offer a cultural treasure chest from which English-speaking peoples have been drawing, in one way or another, for more than three and a half centuries. Folks have been following the advice given in *Kiss Me Kate* – brushing up on their Shakespeare – for quite some time.

But Shakespeare's presence is also reflected in a number of other ways. Consider, for example, the more than 800 operatic and symphonic compositions deriving from such plays as *The Merry Wives of Windsor*, *The Taming of the Shrew*, and *Othello*. Or Broadway musicals, such as *The Boys from Syracuse* (a take-off on *The Comedy of Errors*) and *West Side Story* (Leonard Bernstein's New York gang-war updating of *Romeo and Juliet*). Or literary works such as William Faulkner's *The Sound and the Fury*, a sustained allusion to Macbeth's "tomorrow and tomorrow and tomorrow" speech. Here in the United States, Shakespeare has been part of our lives since the earliest days of the republic – even on the frontier, where spinoffs and parodies of Shakespeare helped while away many an hour in the nineteenth century. We've all delighted in the fractured Shakespeare offered up by the Duke and the King in Mark Twain's *Huckleberry Finn*. Ah yes, numerous – but not always sweet – are the uses of Shakespeare.

Nor is there any reason to think that Shakespeare's influence will be any less vital in the future than in the past. In most of the countries of the world, Shakespeare continues to maintain his position as the most frequently performed playwright. Every summer in the United States, for example, Shakespeare festivals highlight the vacation map from Maine to Texas, from Alabama to Oregon.

Ben Jonson was right, then, when he prefaced the first collected edition of Shakespeare's plays with the words "he was not of an age, but for all time!"

The Stratford Years

But if Shakespeare was a man for all time, he was also very much a man of his own age. Christened at Holy Trinity Church in Stratford-upon-Avon in April, 1564, he grew up, the son of illiterate parents, in a small Warwickshire town more noted for its wool and leather goods than for its literary cultivation. His mother, Mary Arden, was the daughter of a well-to-do farmer. His father, John Shakespeare, was a successful glovemaker who held several important borough offices in Stratford before he suffered financial reverses during William's teen years. The birth-place house still stands.

It seems all but certain that young Shakespeare spent most of his weekdays at the nearby Stratford grammar school, where, having learned his ABCs and the Lord's Prayer from a horn-book, he would have gone on to study Latin

Holy Trinity Church, Stratford-on-Avon

Shakespeare's House, Stratford-on-Avon

under the supervision of a stern schoolmaster. Sundays he would have attended religious services, studying the catechism of the newly re-established Church of England and worshiping in accordance with *The Book of Common Prayer.*

It was a rigorous upbringing, and it equipped Shakespeare with enough background to become one of the most widely educated men who ever lived — despite the fact that he never attended a day at a college or university.

Judging from his plays and poems, we may infer that Shakespeare was interested in virtually every aspect of human life — in professions such as law, medicine, religion, and teaching; in everyday occupations such as farming, sheepherding, tailoring, and shopkeeping; in skills such as fishing, gardening, and cooking. Much of what Shakespeare knew about these and countless other subjects he would have acquired from books. He must have been a voracious reader.

But he would have learned a great deal, also, from simply being alert to all that went on around him. He would have observed the plant and animal life of the nearby woods that he would later immortalize, in *As You Like It*, as the Forest of Arden. While there, he may have hunted from time to time; one legend has it that he left Stratford because he had been caught poaching deer from the estate of a powerful squire four miles upstream. He probably learned to swim as a youth, skinny-dipping in the river Avon. He may have participated in the kinds of athletic competition that were popular in the Elizabethan equivalent of the Olympics, the Cotswold Games. Chances are, too, that he would have been familiar with indoor recreations such as hazard (a popular dice game), or chess, or any of a number of card games. His works make it clear that he was fully at home with a broad spectrum of pastimes characteristic of the daily life of Elizabethan England.

Once his schooldays ended, Shakespeare married, at the age of eighteen, a woman who was eight years his senior. Anne Hathaway was pregnant when the wedding vows were solemnized. That it was a forced marriage is unlikely. But we shall never know how close the couple were. What we do know is that a daughter, Susanna, was baptized in Holy Trinity in May of 1583, followed less than two years later by the christening of twins, Hamnet and Judith. Sometime thereafter, certainly by the late 1580s, the father was in London.

The London Years

London was approximately a hundred miles distant. Shakespeare may have traveled there by way of the spires of Oxford, as do most visitors returning from Stratford to London today. But why he went, or when, history does not tell us. It has been plausibly suggested that he joined an acting troupe that was one player short when it toured Stratford in 1587. All we know for certain is that by 1592 Shakespeare had established himself as an actor and had written at least three plays. One of these — the third part of *Henry VI* — was alluded to in that year in a testament by a dying poet and playwright. Robert Greene warned his fellow playwrights to beware of the "upstart crow" who, not content with being a mere player, was aspiring to a share of the livelihood that had previously been the exclusive province of professional writers such as "the University Wits."

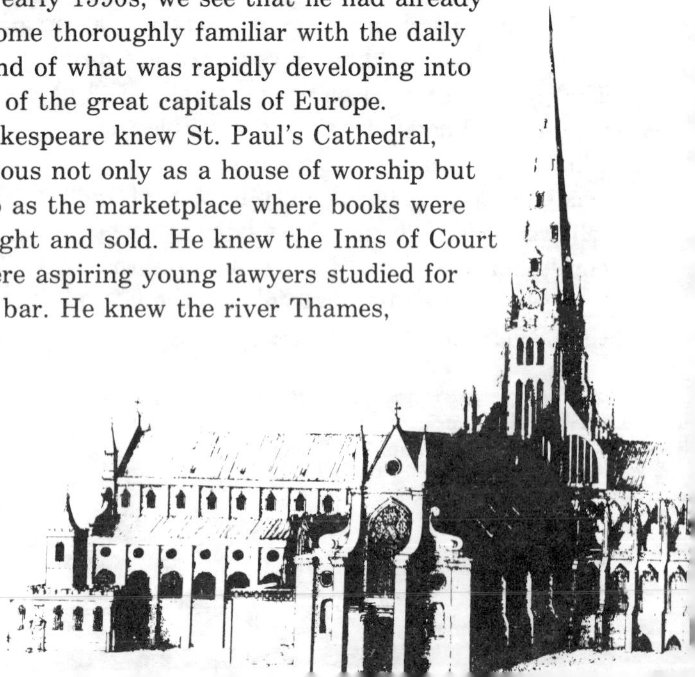

If we look at what Shakespeare had written by the early 1590s, we see that he had already become thoroughly familiar with the daily round of what was rapidly developing into one of the great capitals of Europe. Shakespeare knew St. Paul's Cathedral, famous not only as a house of worship but also as the marketplace where books were bought and sold. He knew the Inns of Court where aspiring young lawyers studied for the bar. He knew the river Thames,

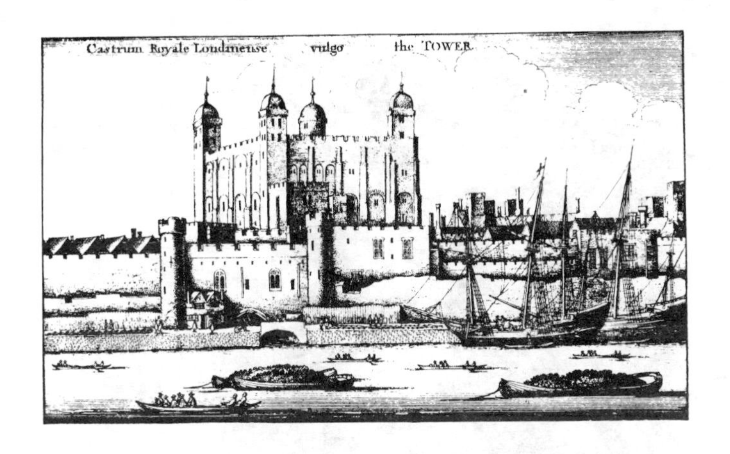

spanned by the ever-busy, ever-fascinating London Bridge. He knew the Tower, where so many of the characters he would depict in his history plays had met their deaths, and where in his own lifetime, such prominent noblemen as the Earl of Essex and Sir Walter Raleigh would be imprisoned prior to their executions. He knew Westminster, where Parliament met when summoned by the Queen, and where the Queen herself kept her court at Whitehall Palace. He knew the harbor, where English ships, having won control of the seas by defeating the "invincible" Spanish Armada in 1588, had begun in earnest to explore the New World.

In Shakespeare's day, London was a vigorous city of approximately 160,000. If in its more majestic aspects it was dominated by the court of Queen Elizabeth — the sovereign most historians regard as the greatest monarch in English history — in its everyday affairs it was accented by the hustle-bustle of getting and spending. Its Royal Exchange was one of the forerunners of today's stock exchanges. Its many marketplaces offered a variety of goods for a variety of tastes.

Its crowded streets presented a colorful pageant of Elizabethan modes of transport and dress, ranging from countrywomen in homespun to elegant ladies in apparel as decorative as their husbands' wealth – and the Queen's edicts on clothing – would allow. Its inns and taverns afforded a robust diversity of vivid personalities—eating, drinking, talking, and enjoying games of all kinds.

London was, in short, a stimulating social and cultural environment for the poet whose works would later be praised as the very "mirror of life." And the young playwright took full advantage of the opportunity to observe humanity in all its facets. Without the broadening that London provided, it is doubtful that Shakespeare could ever have created such breathtakingly real characters as Falstaff, Prince Hal, and "all the good lads in Eastcheap."

Not that all was always well. Like any major city, London also had its unpleasant aspects. For one thing, it was riddled with conflict. Preachers were constantly denouncing the excessive use of cosmetics by women of the period. Even Hamlet speaks out against "your paintings," telling Ophelia "God has given you one face, and you make yourselves another."

In a similar vein, the city's Puritan authorities, regarding the theatres as dens of iniquity, closed them down on any available pretext, particularly during periods when the plague was rampant.

But even with the theatres closed, London was not free of vice and crime. In the Bankside district, prostitution abounded, as did gambling and drunkenness. Pickpockets, vagabonds, and other members of the fraternity of urban lowlife lay in wait for "conies" or unsuspecting victims. With so many "notorious villainies" for the "Belman of London" to bring to light, it is not surprising that some of the most interesting pamphlets of the period were muckraking tracts from reformers outraged by the sinfulness of the modern metropolis.

In such a setting did Shakespeare write and perform the greatest dramatic works the world has ever seen. And he did so in an area of the city that was accustomed to entertainments we would regard as the very antithesis of the sweet Swan of Avon's poetic sublimity. For if Bankside was to blossom into the finest theatrical center of that or any other age, it was also, for better or worse, the seedbed for such crude and cruel spectator sports as bear-baiting, bull-baiting, and cock-fighting. This may help account for the blood and violence one often sees on the Elizabethan stage, even in such Shakespearean works as *Titus Andronicus*, *Julius Caesar*, and *King Lear*.

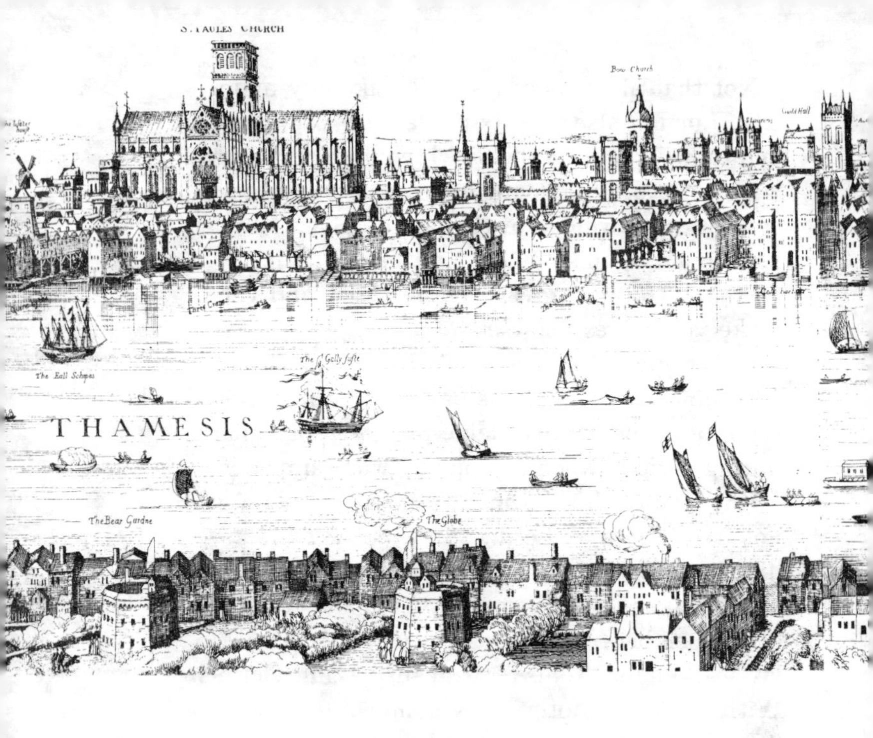

But of course there was more than murder and mayhem in the "wooden O" that served as amphitheatre for Shakespeare's works. On a stage largely devoid of scenery, the playwright and the actor made splendid use of language and gesture to establish locale, atmosphere, and meaning. And because the stage was surrounded on three sides by nearby spectators, the playwright and the actor benefited from a more intimate relationship with the audience than is customary in present-day theatres fitted with a curtain and a proscenium arch. For Shakespeare, this meant that he could allow a character to confide in the audience through asides, as does Iago in *Othello*, or to be overheard as he meditates in solitude, as does Hamlet in his celebrated "To be or not to be" soliloquy.

The limitations of the Globe and similar Elizabethan theatres are obvious to us today. For one thing, they were exposed to the sky and thus could not operate comfortably in inclement weather or in darkness. For another, lacking spotlights and other modern paraphernalia, they could not achieve some of the special effects we have come to take for granted in the theatre of our own day. What we sometimes forget, however, is that these limitations could be liberating for the playwright and the actor, making possible a kind of dramatic invention and flexibility difficult to duplicate in the more "advanced" theatre of the twentieth century.

The same was probably true in the Blackfriars and other private indoor theatres of the period, not to mention the halls at Court or the great palaces of the nobility. For it is well to remember that many of Shakespeare's plays were performed in theatrical settings other than the Globe, or its predecessor, the Theatre, or other amphitheatres of the period. Shakespeare's company was known as the Lord Chamberlain's Men from 1594 to 1603, when Queen Elizabeth died; after the accession of King James I, from 1603 on, it was known as the King's Men. Both designations implied a special relationship with the Court, and Shakespeare and his colleagues were invited to perform before the monarch more often than all the other acting troupes in the realm combined.

Shakespeare's real bread and butter, however, came from the immense cross section of the English populace who thronged to Bankside to see his plays performed. Despite the occasional caviling of such rival playwrights as Ben Jonson (whose admiration for Shakespeare was at times "this side idolatry"), we have reason to believe

Interior of Holy Trinity Church

that Shakespeare's dramatic works were immediately recognized for their artistic merits. By 1598, a critic named Francis Meres was comparing Shakespeare's genius to that of the greatest poets of antiquity – Ovid, Plautus, and Seneca – and finding the contemporary playwright superior to his classical predecessors. But unlike many great writers, Shakespeare was also a popular success in his own lifetime. He earned a generous amount of money, invested it wisely in real estate, both in London and in Stratford, and around 1613, eased into a gentleman's retirement – the owner of New Place, the second largest house in his native town.

There, three years later, he died. Fittingly, his death date, like the date tradition has agreed upon for his birth date, was April 23, the day England celebrated its patron saint. In the four centuries since the poet's birth, it seems no exaggeration to say that he has eclipsed even the heroic St. George in glory.

Epilogue

Shakespeare was laid to rest where fifty-two years earlier he had been christened. Shortly thereafter, a monument to his memory was erected above the tomb in Holy Trinity, and that monument is still in place for Shakespeare admirers to see today. But an even greater monument to his memory was produced several years later, when his theatrical colleagues assembled a large volume of his plays. The First Folio of 1623 was a labor of love, compiled as "an office to the dead, to procure his orphans' guardians" and "to keep the memory of so worthy a friend and fellow alive as was our Shakespeare." To that end, it was an unparalleled success, a publication that has aptly been summed up as "incomparably the most important work in the English language."

Among other things, the First Folio preserves what is generally considered the most reliable portrait of Shakespeare, the title-page engraving by Martin Droeshout. In dedicatory verses opposite the portrait, Ben Jonson attests to its authenticity. But quite properly, he then goes on to observe that though the engraver has "hit his face," he has been unable to draw "his wit." For that — for the mastery of language, of character, of poetic drama, of all that reminds us that, after all is said and done, "the play's the thing" — Jonson tells the reader, "look not on his picture but his book."

And so, for more than three and a half centuries, we have. We have read, and studied, and memorized, and performed — and yes, we have worshiped — the man Jonson praised as "Soul of the Age! The applause, delight, the wonder of our stage!"

Bardolatry — the word we use to refer to Shakespeare-worship — has had many manifestations over the intervening centuries. It has animated hundreds of Shakespeare festivals and celebrations, of which undoubtedly the most famous was the great Shakespeare Jubilee of 1769. On that occasion, thousands braved rainy Stratford weather to participate in ceremonies presided over by the principal actor of the eighteenth century, David Garrick. In a somewhat inverted form, Bardolatry has given rise to the notion that someone other than the son of ill-educated, small-town parents wrote the plays we attribute to William Shakespeare. Hence Francis Bacon, the Earl of Oxford, and other members of the nobility have been proposed as the "true" author of the works we still securely hold to be Shakespeare's. And Bardolatry has also occasioned an unceasing cavalcade of Shakespearean curios and knickknacks: everything from ceramic figurines and mulberry-wood chests to Shakespeare-lovers' poker cloths and Superbard T-shirts.

On the more serious side, appreciation of Shakespeare has inspired notable works of art by painters as diverse as Thomas Rowlandson, George Romney, Henry Fuseli, Eugene Delacroix, George Cruikshank, Arthur Rackham, Pablo Picasso, Salvador Dali, and David Hockney. His works have provided the basis of hundreds of musical tributes, by composers ranging from Beethoven to Mendelssohn, Tchaikovsky to Verdi. And of course his plays continue to be performed in theatres, in movie houses, and on television screens.

The Bard is in our bones. Shakespeare lives.

John F. Andrews
Former Editor Shakespeare Quarterly
Folger Shakespeare Library

OOD FREND FOR IESVS SAKE FORBEARE,
O DIGG THE DVST ENCLOASED HEARE.
LESE BE YE MAN YT SPARES THES STONES
ND CVRST BE HE YT MOVES MY BONES.

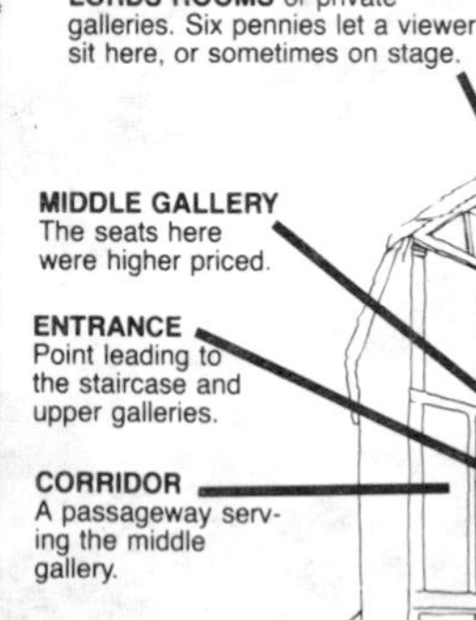

LORDS ROOMS or private galleries. Six pennies let a viewer sit here, or sometimes on stage.
FLAG
A white flag above the theater meant a show that day.
HUT
A storage area that also he
a winch system for lowering
characters to the stage.
MIDDLE GALLERY
The seats here were higher priced.
TRAP DOOR
Leading to the Hell area where a winch elevator was located.
THE HEAVENS
So identified by being
painted with the zodiac s
WARDROBE
An essential storage are
GALLERY
Located above the st
to house musicians c
spectators.
ENTRANCE
Point leading to the staircase and upper galleries.
CORRIDOR
A passageway serv- ing the middle gallery.
DRESSING ROOMS
Rooms where actors were 'attired' and awaited their cues.
INNER STAGE
A recessed playing a
often curtained off
except as needed.
MAIN ENTRANCE
Here the doorkeeper collected penny admission.
TIRING-HOUSE DOC
The rear entrance or
'stage door' for actors
or privileged spectato
THE PIT
Sometimes referred to as 'The Yard' where the 'groundlings' watched.
TIRING-HOUSE
Backstage area pro- vided space for storage and business
STAGE
Major playing area jutting into the Pit, creating a sense of intimacy.
HELL
The area under the stage, used for ghostly comings and goings or for storage.
STAIRS
Theatergoers reached the galleries by staircases enclosed by stairwells.
STAGE DOORS
Doors opening into the Tiring-House

A Midsummer Night's Dream

DRAMATIS PERSONAE

THESEUS, *duke of Athens.*
EGEUS, *father to Hermia.*
LYSANDER, *betrothed to Hermia.*
DEMETRIUS, *in love with Hermia.*
PHILOSTRATE, *master of the revels to Theseus.*

HIPPOLYTA, *queen of the Amazons, betrothed to Theseus.*
HERMIA, *daughter to Egeus, betrothed to Lysander.*
HELENA, *in love with Demetrius.*

<table>
<tr><td>QUINCE, a carpenter,
BOTTOM, a weaver,
FLUTE, a bellows-mender,
SNOUT, a tinker,
SNUG, a joiner,
STARVELING, a tailor,</td><td>presenting</td><td>PROLOGUE.
PYRAMUS.
THISBE.
WALL.
LION.
MOONSHINE.</td></tr>
</table>

OBERON, *king of the fairies.*
TITANIA, *queen of the fairies.*
ROBIN GOODFELLOW, *a Puck.*

<table>
<tr><td>PEASEBLOSSOM,
COBWEB,
MOTH,
MUSTARDSEED,</td><td>fairies.</td></tr>
</table>

Other fairies attending their King and Queen.
Attendants on Theseus and Hippolyta.

SCENE: *Athens, and a wood near it.*

A Midsummer Night's Dream

Characters

THESEUS, *duke of Athens.*
EGEUS, *father of Hermia.*
LYSANDER, *betrothed to Hermia.*
DEMETRIUS, *in love with Hermia.*
PHILOSTRATE, *master of Theseus' revels.*

HIPPOLYTA, *queen of the Amazons, betrothed to Theseus.*
HERMIA, *daughter of Egeus, betrothed to Lysander.*
HELENA, *in love with Demetrius.*

	also plays	
PETER QUINCE, *a carpenter*		PROLOGUE.
NICK BOTTOM, *a weaver*		PYRAMUS.
FRANCIS FLUTE, *a bellows mender*		THISBY.
TOM SNOUT, *a tinker*		WALL.
SNUG, *a joiner*		LION.
ROBIN STARVELING, *a tailor*		MOONSHINE.

OBERON, *king of the Fairies.*
TITANIA, *queen of the Fairies.*
PUCK *or* ROBIN GOODFELLOW.
PEASEBLOSSOM,
COBWEB,
MOTH,
MUSTARDSEED, } *fairies.*

Other fairies attending Oberon and Titania.
Attendants on Theseus and Hippolyta.

Scene: Athens and a nearby wood.

Act I, Scene i: [*Athens. The Palace of Theseus.*] *Enter* THESEUS, HIPPOLYTA, PHILOSTRATE, *with others.*

THESEUS
Now, fair Hippolyta, our nuptial hour
Draws on apace. Four happy days bring in
Another moon; but, O, methinks, how slow
This old moon wanes! She lingers my desires,
5 Like to a step-dame or a dowager
Long withering out a young man's revenue.

HIPPOLYTA
Four days will quickly steep themselves in night;
Four nights will quickly dream away the time;
And then the moon, like to a silver bow
10 New-bent in heaven, shall behold the night
Of our solemnities.

THESEUS
Go, Philostrate,
Stir up the Athenian youth to merriments;
Awake the pert and nimble spirit of mirth;
15 Turn melancholy forth to funerals.
The pale companion is not for our pomp.
[*Exit* PHILOSTRATE.]
Hippolyta, I woo'd thee with my sword,
And won thy love doing thee injuries;
But I will wed thee in another key,
20 With pomp, with triumph, and with revelling.
Enter EGEUS, HERMIA, LYSANDER, *and* DEMETRIUS.

---

17 *woo'd thee with my sword* Theseus captured Hippolyta when he conquered the Amazons. She was the Amazon queen.

Act I, Scene i: The palace of Theseus. Enter THESEUS, HIPPOLYTA, PHILOSTRATE, *and others.*

THESEUS
Now, beautiful Hippolyta, our wedding hour
quickly approaches. In four happy days we'll see
another moon, but, oh, how slowly
the old moon fades. She prolongs my desires
5 like a stepmother or a widow
who drains away a young man's income.

HIPPOLYTA
Four days will quickly become immersed in night.
Four nights will quickly dream away the time,
and then the moon, like a silver bow
10 newly bent in heaven, will witness the night
of our wedding ceremony.

THESEUS
Go, Philostrate,
stir up the young people of Athens to festivities.
Wake up the lively and nimble spirit of fun.
15 Show melancholy the way to the funerals.
That sad fellow is not welcome at our happy festival.
PHILOSTRATE *exits.*
Hippolyta, I pursued you with my sword,
and I won your love as I was giving you injury.
But I will marry you in a different tone,
20 with ceremony, pageantry, and celebration.
Enter EGEUS, *his daughter* HERMIA, LYSANDER, *and* DEMETRIUS.

EGEUS

Happy be Theseus, our renownèd Duke!

THESEUS

Thanks, good Egeus; what's the news with thee?

EGEUS

Full of vexation come I, with complaint
Against my child, my daughter Hermia.
25 Stand forth, Demetrius. My noble lord,
This man hath my consent to marry her.
Stand forth, Lysander: and, my gracious Duke,
This man hath bewitch'd the bosom of my child.
Thou, thou, Lysander, thou hast given her rhymes
30 And interchang'd love-tokens with my child.
Thou hast by moonlight at her window sung
With faining voice verses of faining love,
And stol'n the impression of her fantasy
With bracelets of thy hair, rings, gawds, conceits,
35 Knacks, trifles, nosegays, sweetmeats,—messengers
Of strong prevailment in unhard'ned youth.
With cunning hast thou filch'd my daughter's heart,
Turn'd her obedience, which is due to me,
To stubborn harshness; and, my gracious Duke,
40 Be it so she will not here before your Grace
Consent to marry with Demetrius,
I beg the ancient privilege of Athens,
As she is mine, I may dispose of her;
Which shall be either to this gentleman
45 Or to her death, according to our law
Immediately provided in that case.

THESEUS

What say you, Hermia? Be advis'd, fair maid.
To you your father should be as a god,
One that compos'd your beauties, yea, and one
50 To whom you are but as a form in wax
By him imprinted, and within his power
To leave the figure or disfigure it.
Demetrius is a worthy gentleman.

EGEUS
I wish you happiness, Theseus, our famous duke.

THESEUS
Thank you, good Egeus. What's your news?

EGEUS
I come to you full of troubles. I have a complaint
against my child, my daughter Hermia.
25 Come here, Demetrius. My noble lord,
this man has my consent to marry her.
Come here, Lysander. And my gracious lord,
this man has ensnared the heart of my child.
You, you, Lysander, you have given her poems
30 and you have exchanged tokens of love with my child.
At moonlight by her window, you've sung
seductive love poems in a seductive voice.
You have deviously captured her imagination
with bracelets of your hair, rings, trinkets, clever baubles,
35 knickknacks, trifles, flowers, candy—all messengers
of strong persuasion for an innocent young woman.
With cunning you have stolen my daughter's heart
and turned the obedience due to me
to stubborn harshness. So, my gracious duke,
40 if she will not consent, here before you, your grace,
to agree to marry Demetrius,
I beg to be granted the ancient privilege of Athens.
That states that since she is mine, I can deliver her
either to this gentleman (Demetrius)
45 or to her death, according to the law
which is expressly granted in this case.

THESEUS
What do you say, Hermia? Listen to me, lovely maiden:
To you, your father should be like a god,
one who created your beauty. Yes, and one
50 to whom you are just a wax form
which he formed and which he can
leave untouched or destroy.
Demetrius is a worthy gentleman.

HERMIA
So is Lysander.

THESEUS
55 In himself he is;
But in this kind, wanting your father's voice,
The other must be held the worthier.

HERMIA
I would my father look'd but with my eyes.

THESEUS
Rather your eyes must with his judgement look.

HERMIA
60 I do entreat your Grace to pardon me.
I know not by what power I am made bold,
Nor how it may concern my modesty,
In such a presence here to plead my thoughts;
But I beseech your Grace that I may know
65 The worst that may befall me in this case,
If I refuse to wed Demetrius.

THESEUS
Either to die the death or to abjure
For ever the society of men.
Therefore, fair Hermia, question your desires,
70 Know of your youth, examine well your blood,
Whether, if you yield not to your father's choice,
You can endure the livery of a nun,
For aye to be in shady cloister mew'd,
To live a barren sister all your life,
75 Chanting faint hymns to the cold fruitless moon.
Thrice-blessed they that master so their blood
To undergo such maiden pilgrimage;
But earthlier happy is the rose distill'd
Than that which withering on the virgin thorn
80 Grows, lives, and dies in single blessedness.

HERMIA
So will I grow, so live, so die, my lord,
Ere I will yield my virgin patent up

HERMIA
So is Lysander.

THESEUS
55 Yes, in himself he his.
But in this case, since your father does not approve of him,
the other man must be considered worthier.

HERMIA
I only wish my father could see with my eyes.

THESEUS
To the contrary, you must judge things from his viewpoint.

HERMIA
60 I beg your grace to pardon me.
I don't know what influence makes me so bold,
or how it will compromise my reputation for modesty
to plead for my thoughts in such company.
But, I beg you, your grace, that I may know
65 the worst that can happen to me in this situation
if I refuse to marry Demetrius.

THESEUS
You must either die or give up
forever the society of men.
Therefore, beautiful Hermia, closely examine your desires,
70 think about your youth, examine your passions.
Decide whether or not, if you don't choose the man your
father favors,
you can stand to wear the clothing of a nun.
You will be shut up in a dark convent forever
to live as a childless sister all your life,
75 chanting weak hymns to the cold, childless moon.
Three-times blessed are those who can control their
passions to such a degree
and choose such a virginal route.
But the rose that is picked for perfume is happier in
earthly terms
than the rose that withers on the untouched vine—
80 which grows, lives, and dies in lonely purity.

HERMIA
Then that is the way I will grow, live, and die, my lord,
before I will give up my right to virginity

Unto his lordship, whose unwished yoke
My soul consents not to give sovereignty.

THESEUS

85 Take time to pause; and, by the next new moon—
The sealing-day betwixt my love and me
For everlasting bond of fellowship—
Upon that day either prepare to die
For disobedience to your father's will,
90 Or else to wed Demetrius, as he would,
Or on Diana's altar to protest
For aye austerity and single life.

DEMETRIUS

Relent, sweet Hermia; and, Lysander, yield
Thy crazed title to my certain right.

LYSANDER

95 You have her father's love, Demetrius,
Let me have Hermia's; do you marry him.

EGEUS

Scornful Lysander! true, he hath my love,
And what is mine my love shall render him.
And she is mine, and all my right of her
100 I do estate unto Demetrius.

LYSANDER

I am, my lord, as well deriv'd as he,
As well possess'd; my love is more than his;
My fortunes every way as fairly rank'd,
If not with vantage, as Demetrius';
105 And, which is more than all these boasts can be,
I am belov'd of beauteous Hermia.
Why should not I then prosecute my right?
Demetrius, I'll avouch it to his head,
Made love to Nedar's daughter, Helena,
110 And won her soul; and she, sweet lady, dotes,
Devoutly dotes, dotes in idolatry,
Upon this spotted and inconstant man.

and put it in the hands of that lord to whose unwelcome proposal
my soul will not consent to acknowledge as my master.

THESEUS
85 Take time to think it over, and by the next new moon—
the day my love and I will seal our love
in the everlasting bond of marriage—
upon that day, either prepare to die
for disobeying your father's orders,
90 or else marry Demetrius as your father wishes.
If not, you must vow on Diana's altar
to live forever an austere and unmarried life.

DEMETRIUS
Give in, sweet Hermia. Lysander, give up
your weak claim to my undeniable right.

LYSANDER
95 You have her father's love, Demetrius.
Let me have Hermia's. You can marry him.

EGEUS
Scornful Lysander! You're right, I do love him;
and my love shall give him what is mine.
And Hermia is mine, and all my rights to her,
100 I give to Demetrius.

LYSANDER
My lord, my family is as noble as his,
and just as rich; my love is greater than his.
My fortunes are in every way equal,
if not better, than Demetrius'.
105 And what is more important than all of these boasts is that
I am loved by the beautiful Hermia.
Why shouldn't I claim my rights then?
I will swear it to his face that Demetrius
made love to Nedar's daughter, Helena,
110 and won her heart. And she, sweet lady, adores him—
devoutly adores him, adores him to the point of idolizing him—
this immoral and unfaithful man.

THESEUS

I must confess that I have heard so much,
And with Demetrius thought to have spoke thereof;
115 But, being over-full of self-affairs,
My mind did lose it. But, Demetrus, come;
And come, Egeus; you shall go with me;
I have some private schooling for you both.
For you, fair Hermia, look you arm yourself
120 To fit your fancies to your father's will;
Or else the law of Athens yields you up—
Which by no means we may extenuate—
To death, or to a vow of single life.
Come, my Hippolyta; what cheer, my love?
125 Demetrius and Egeus, go along.
I must employ you in some business
Against our nuptial, and confer with you
Of something nearly that concerns yourselves.

EGEUS

With duty and desire we follow you.
[*Exeunt all but* LYSANDER *and* HERMIA.]

LYSANDER

130 How now, my love! why is your cheek so pale?
How chance the roses there do fade so fast?

HERMIA

Belike for want of rain, which I could well
Beteem them from the tempest of my eyes.

LYSANDER

Ay me! for aught that I could ever read,
135 Could ever hear by tale or history,
The course of true love never did run smooth;
But, either it was different in blood,—

HERMIA

O cross! too high to be enthrall'd to low.

LYSANDER

Or else misgraffed in respect of years,—

THESEUS

I must confess that I have heard that,
and I had meant to speak with Demetrius about it.
15 But, being overly concerned with my own affairs,
I forgot. But come, Demetrius;
and come, Egeus. You shall go with me.
I want to pass along some information to you in private.
As for you, beautiful Hermia, see that you prepare
yourself
20 to adapt your love to your father's orders.
If not, the law of Athens decrees that you must face—
and by no means can I lessen the sentence—
death or an unmarried life as a nun.
Come, my Hippolyta. What do you say, my love?
25 Demetrius and Egeus, come along.
I must ask you to do some things
to prepare for our wedding, and I need to confer with you
about something of importance to you.

EGEUS

We follow you with eager obedience.

All exit, except LYSANDER *and* HERMIA.

LYSANDER

30 What's wrong, my love? Why are you so pale?
Why do the roses fade so fast from your cheeks?

HERMIA

Perhaps it is for lack of rain, which I could easily
give them with a storm from my eyes.

LYSANDER

Alas! Nothing that I have ever read
35 or have ever heard from stories and from history
said that the course of true love runs smoothly.
But either because of a difference in rank—

HERMIA

O, what a misfortune! Too noble to be enslaved by such a
humble lover!

LYSANDER

Or else be mismatched in terms of age—

HERMIA
140 O spite! too old to be engag'd to young.

LYSANDER
Or else it stood upon the choice of friends,—

HERMIA
O hell! to choose love by another's eyes.

LYSANDER
Or, if there were a sympathy in choice,
War, death, or sickness did lay siege to it,
145 Making it momentany as a sound,
Swift as a shadow, short as any dream,
Brief as the lightning in the collied night,
That, in a spleen, unfolds both heaven and earth,
And ere a man hath power to say "Behold!"
150 The jaws of darkness do devour it up:
So quick bright things come to confusion.

HERMIA
If then true lovers have been ever cross'd,
It stands as an edict in destiny.
Then let us teach our trial patience,
155 Because it is a customary cross,
As due to love as thoughts and dreams and sighs,
Wishes and tears, poor Fancy's followers.

LYSANDER
A good persuasion; therefore, hear me, Hermia.
I have a widow aunt, a dowager
160 Of great revenue, and she hath no child.
From Athens is her house remote seven leagues;
And she respects me as her only son.
There, gentle Hermia, may I marry thee;
And to that place the sharp Athenian law
165 Cannot pursue us. If thou lov'st me then,
Steal forth thy father's house to-morrow night;
And in the wood, a league without the town,
Where I did meet thee once with Helena
To do observance to a morn of May,
170 There will I stay for thee.

HERMIA

140 O spite! Too old to be engaged to one so young!

LYSANDER

Or else because of the opinion of friends—

HERMIA

O hell! To choose a lover by someone else's standards!

LYSANDER

Or else if they are well matched,
war, death, or sickness would seize it
145 and make it as momentary as a sound,
as swift as a shadow, as short as any dream,
or as brief as lightning on a dark night
that in a flash, reveals both heaven and earth.
And before a man has the power to say, "Behold,"
150 the jaws of darkness have swallowed it.
Just in that manner do all quick, bright things come to a
dark end.

HERMIA

If true lovers have always been afflicted,
it is because fate orders it.
So let us learn to be patient in our suffering
155 because suffering is a normal cross to bear.
It is as much a part of love as thoughts and dreams and
sighs,
and wishes and tears—poor love's followers.

LYSANDER

That's a wise point of view. So listen, Hermia.
I have a widowed aunt, an heiress,
160 with a large income and no children.
Her house is about twenty-one miles from Athens,
and she thinks of me as her only son.
There, gentle Hermia, I can marry you.
There the strict Athenian law
165 cannot follow us. If you love me, then,
sneak out of your father's house tomorrow night.
In the woods, about three miles outside of town,
where I once met you with Helena
to take part in the May Day celebration,
170 I will wait for you.

HERMIA

My good Lysander!
I swear to thee, by Cupid's strongest bow,
By his best arrow with the golden head,
By the simplicity of Venus' doves,
175 By that which knitteth souls and prospers loves,
And by that fire which burn'd the Carthage queen
When the false Troyan under sail was seen,
By all the vows that ever men have broke,
In number more than ever women spoke,
180 In that same place thou hast appointed me
To-morrow truly will I meet with thee.

LYSANDER

Keep promise, love. Look, here comes Helena.

Enter HELENA.

HERMIA

God speed fair Helena! Whither away?

HELENA

Call you me fair? That fair again unsay.
185 Demetrius loves your fair, O happy fair!
Your eyes are lode-stars, and your tongue's sweet air
More tuneable than lark to shepherd's ear
When wheat is green, when hawthorn buds appear.
Sickness is catching; O, were favour so,
190 Yours would I catch, fair Hermia, ere I go;
My ear should catch your voice, my eye your eye,
My tongue should catch your tongue's sweet melody.
Were the world mine, Demetrius being bated,
The rest I'll give to be to you translated.
195 O, teach me how you look, and with what art
You sway the motion of Demetrius' heart.

HERMIA

I frown upon him, yet he loves me still.

HELENA

O that your frowns would teach my smiles such skill!

---

172 *Cupid* Roman god of love. Struck by one of Cupid's gold-tipped arrows, a man or woman immediately fell in love. A lead-tipped arrow caused hate. 176 *Carthage queen* Dido, who committed suicide when she saw that Aeneas, her lover, had left her.

HERMIA

My good Lysander!
I swear to you, by Cupid's strongest bow,
by his best arrow with the golden head,
by the innocence of Venus' doves,
175 by that which binds up souls and furthers love,
and by the fire which burned the Carthage queen
when that fickle Trojan Aeneas set sail—
by all the vows that men have ever broken
(which are more numerous than women have ever spoken),
180 in that place that you have set for meeting me,
I swear I'll meet you tomorrow.

LYSANDER

Keep your promise, love. Look, here comes Helena.
Enter HELENA.

HERMIA

God bless you, lovely Helena. Where are you going?

HELENA

Do you call me beautiful? Take back that "beautiful."
185 Demetrius loves your beauty. O happy beautiful one!
Your eyes are guiding stars, and your voice is sweet music,
more tuneful than a lark to a shepherd's ear
when wheat is green and hawthorn buds appear.
Sickness is catching. O, if only looks were catching,
190 I would catch yours, Hermia, before I left!
My ear would catch your voice, my eye would catch your eye,
my tongue would catch your voice's sweet melody.
If all the world were mine, except for Demetrius,
I'd give it all to be changed into you.
195 O, teach me to look like you and the tricks
with which you captured Demetrius' heart!

HERMIA

I frown at him, yet he still loves me.

HELENA

I wish your frowns could teach my smiles such skill!

HERMIA
I give him curses, yet he gives me love.

HELENA
200 O that my prayers could such affection move!

HERMIA
The more I hate, the more he follows me.

HELENA
The more I love, the more he hateth me.

HERMIA
His folly, Helena, is no fault of mine.

HELENA
None, but your beauty. Would that fault were mine!

HERMIA
205 Take comfort; he no more shall see my face;
Lysander and myself will fly this place.
Before the time I did Lysander see,
Seem'd Athens as a paradise to me;
O, then, what graces in my love do dwell,
210 That he hath turn'd a heaven unto a hell!

LYSANDER
Helen, to you our minds we will unfold.
To-morrow night, when Phoebe doth behold
Her silver visage in the wat'ry glass,
Decking with liquid pearl the bladed grass,
215 A time that lovers' flights doth still conceal,
Through Athens' gates have we devis'd to steal.

HERMIA
And in the wood, where often you and I
Upon faint primrose-beds were wont to lie,
Emptying our bosoms of their counsel sweet.
220 There my Lysander and myself shall meet;
And thence from Athens turn away our eyes,
To seek new friends and stranger companies.
Farewell, sweet playfellow! Pray thou for us;
And good luck grant thee thy Demetrius!

---

212 *Phoebe* the goddess of the moon.

HERMIA
I give him curses, yet he gives me love.

HELENA
200 I wish my prayers could win me such affection!

HERMIA
The more I hate him, the more he follows me.

HELENA
The more I love him, the more he hates me.

HERMIA
Helena, his foolishness is not my fault.

HELENA
No—except for your beauty. I wish I had that fault!

HERMIA
205 Take comfort. He shall not see my face again.
Lysander and I are going to flee from this place.
Before I met Lysander,
Athens seemed like a paradise to me.
But my lover is filled with such graces
210 that he has turned a heaven into a hell.

LYSANDER
Helen, we will tell you our secret plans.
Tomorrow night, when Phoebe can see
her silvery face in the water's mirror
and she dresses the blades of grass in liquid pearls,
215 —a time when lovers' flights are always hidden—
we are going to sneak out of Athens' gates.

HERMIA
And in the woods, where often you and I
used to lie upon pale primrose beds
telling each other everything in our secret hearts,
220 Lysander and I will meet.
We shall turn our eyes away from Athens
and find new friends among strangers.
Goodbye, sweet playmate. Pray for us.
And I hope that you are fortunate in winning your
Demetrius!

225 Keep word, Lysander; we must starve our sight
From lovers' food till morrow deep midnight.

LYSANDER

I will, my Hermia.

[*Exit* HERMIA.]

Helena, adieu:

As you on him, Demetrius dote on you!

[*Exit*.]

HELENA

230 How happy some o'er other some can be!
Through Athens I am thought as fair as she.
But what of that? Demetrius thinks not so;
He will not know what all but he do know;
And as he errs, doting on Hermia's eyes,
235 So I, admiring of his qualities.
Things base and vile, holding no quantity,
Love can transpose to form and dignity.
Love looks not with the eyes but with the mind,
And therefore is wing'd Cupid painted blind.
240 Nor hath Love's mind of any judgement taste;
Wings and no eyes figure unheedy haste;
And therefore is Love said to be a child,
Because in choice he is so oft beguil'd.
As waggish boys in game themselves forswear,
245 So the boy Love is perjur'd every where:
For ere Demetrius look'd on Hermia's eyne,
He hail'd down oaths that he was only mine;
And when this hail some heat from Hermia felt,
So he dissolv'd, and show'rs of oaths did melt.
250 I will go tell him of fair Hermia's flight;
Then to the wood will he to-morrow night
Pursue her; and for this intelligence
If I have thanks, it is a dear expense.
But herein mean I to enrich my pain,
255 To have his sight thither and back again.

[*Exit*.]

225 Keep your word, Lysander. We must starve our eyes
of the sight of each other until tomorrow at dark
midnight.

LYSANDER
I will, my Hermia.
HERMIA *exits.*
Goodbye, Helena.
May Demetrius love you as you love him.
LYSANDER *exits.*

HELENA
230 How happy some people can be in comparison to others.
People all over Athens think I am as beautiful as she.
But what of that? Demetrius doesn't think so.
He refuses to know what everyone except he knows.
And as he makes a mistake, adoring Hermia's eyes,
235 so I make a mistake, admiring all of his characteristics.
Things can be worthless, ugly, and unattractive,
and love can change them to beauty and dignity.
Love doesn't look with his eyes, but with his mind,
and that is why winged Cupid is pictured blind.
240 Love's mind doesn't have a scrap of judgment, either—
wings and no eyes symbolize thoughtless haste.
And, therefore, Love is said to be a child
because in making his choices, he is so often misled.
Just as playful boys in fun lie,
245 so the boy, Love, is perjured everywhere.
For before Demetrius looked in Hermia's eyes,
he hailed down vows that he loved me only.
But when his hail felt some of Hermia's heat,
he dissolved and his shower of vows melted.
250 I will go tell him of beautiful Hermia's flight.
Then to the woods tomorrow night, he will
follow her. And for this information,
if he thanks me, Demetrius will consider it a heavy cost.
But I'll be repaid for my pain
255 by just the sight of him going and coming back again.
Exit.

Act I, Scene ii: [*Athens. Quince's house.*] *Enter* QUINCE, SNUG, BOTTOM, FLUTE, SNOUT, *and* STARVELING.

QUINCE
Is all our company here?

BOTTOM
You were best to call them generally, man by man, according to the scrip.

QUINCE
Here is the scroll of every man's name, which is thought fit,
5 through all Athens, to play in our interlude before the Duke and the Duchess, on his wedding-day at night.

BOTTOM
First, good Peter Quince, say what the play treats on, then read the names of the actors, and so grow to a point.

QUINCE
Marry, our play is *The most lamentable comedy, and most cruel*
10 *death of Pyramus and Thisby.*

BOTTOM
A very good piece of work, I assure you, and a merry. Now, good Peter Quince, call forth your actors by the scroll. Masters, spread yourselves.

QUINCE
Answer as I call you. Nick Bottom, the weaver.

BOTTOM
15 Ready. Name what part I am for, and proceed.

QUINCE
You, Nick Bottom, are set down for Pyramus.

BOTTOM
What is Pyramus? A lover, or a tyrant?

QUINCE
A lover, that kills himself most gallant for love.

BOTTOM
That will ask some tears in the true performing of it. If I do it,

---

2 *generally* Bottom's malapropism (unintentionally humorous substitution of one word for another) for "severally" or "individually." 9 *Marry* exclamation coming from the oath "by the Virgin Mary"; meaning "indeed" or "really." 10 *Pyramus and Thisby* two Babylonian lovers. Their story is similar to Romeo and Juliet's.

Act I, Scene ii: Quince's house. Enter QUINCE, *the carpenter;* SNUG, *the joiner;* BOTTOM, *the weaver;* FLUTE, *the bellows mender;* SNOUT, *the tinker; and* STARVELING, *the tailor.*

QUINCE
Is all of our company here?

BOTTOM
You'd better call them generally man by man according to the script.

QUINCE
Here is a list of every man's name who is considered fit,
5 throughout all of Athens, to play in our drama before the duke and duchess, on their wedding day at night.

BOTTOM
First, good Peter Quince, tell us what the play is about, then read the names of the actors. Come to the point in that way.

QUINCE
Very well, our play is called, *The most lamentable comedy and most cruel*
10 *death of Pyramus and Thisby.*

BOTTOM
It's a very good piece of work, I assure you, and a funny one. Now, good
Peter Quince, call forward your actors from your list. Masters, spread
out.

QUINCE
Answer as I call your name. Nick Bottom, the weaver.

BOTTOM
15 Ready. Tell me what part I have and proceed.

QUINCE
You, Nick Bottom, are set down to play Pyramus.

BOTTOM
Who is Pyramus? A lover or a tyrant?

QUINCE
He is a lover who kills himself most gallantly for love.

BOTTOM
That will call for some tears in an honest performance of the part. If I do it,

20 let the audience look to their eyes. I will move storms, I will condole in some measure. To the rest. Yet my chief humour is for a tyrant. I could play Ercles rarely, or a part to tear a cat in, to make all split.

"The raging rocks
25 And shivering shocks
Shall break the locks
Of prison gates;
And Phibbus' car
Shall shine from far
30 And make and mar
The foolish Fates."

This was lofty! Now name the rest of the players. This is Ercles' vein, a tyrant's vein; a lover is more condoling.

QUINCE
Francis Flute, the bellows-mender.

FLUTE
35 Here, Peter Quince.

QUINCE
Flute, you must take Thisby on you.

FLUTE
What is Thisby? A wand'ring knight?

QUINCE
It is the lady that Pyramus must love.

FLUTE
Nay, faith, let not me play a woman; I have a beard coming.

QUINCE
40 That's all one; you shall play it in a mask, and you may speak as small as you will.

BOTTOM
An I may hide my face, let me play Thisby too. I'll speak in a monstrous little voice, "Thisne! Thisne! Ah Pyramus, my lover dear! thy Thisby dear, and lady dear!"

QUINCE
45 No, no; you must play Pyramus; and, Flute, you Thisby.

---

22 *tyrant* a type of character found in medieval and Renaissance plays. A typical tyrant, like the character Hercules, was a violent ranter. 28 *Phibbus* Bottom's malapropism for Phoebus, the sun god. The god's chariot is the sun. 31 *Fates* three goddesses who deter-

20 let the audience watch out for their eyes! I will move them to storms; I will
grieve to some degree. Go on with your list—yet my best talent is
for playing a tyrant. I could play Hercules beautifully, or any part which calls for ranting,
to make all ears split.

The raging rocks
25 And shivering shocks
Will break the locks
Of prison gates.
And Phibbus' car
Will shine from afar
30 And make and deface
The foolish Fates.

That was topnotch! Now name the rest of the players. That was right in the vein of Hercules—
the vein of a tyrant. A lover is more sympathetic.

QUINCE
Francis Flute, the bellows mender.

FLUTE
35 Here, Peter Quince.

QUINCE
Flute, you must play Thisby.

FLUTE
Who is Thisby? A wandering knight?

QUINCE
She is the lady Pyramus loves.

FLUTE
No, really, don't make me play a woman. I'm growing a beard.

QUINCE
40 That makes no difference. You'll play the part in a mask, and you should speak
as softly as possible.

BOTTOM
If I can hide my face in a mask, let me play Thisby, too. I'll speak in a
monstrously little voice, "Thisne, Thisne!"—"Ah, Pyramus, my dear
lover! I'm your dear Thisby, your dear lady!"

QUINCE
45 No, no! You must play Pyramus, and Flute must play Thisby.

---

mined the fate of humans. Clotho spun the thread of each individual's fate; Lachesis decided each man's lot; and Atropos broke the thread of life. 43 *Thisne* may mean "in this way" or may be Bottom's imitation of Thisby's high, soft voice.

BOTTOM
Well, proceed.

QUINCE
Robin Starveling, the tailor.

STARVELING
Here, Peter Quince.

QUINCE
Robin Starveling, you must play Thisby's mother. Tom Snout,
50 the tinker.

SNOUT
Here, Peter Quince.

QUINCE
You, Pyramus' father; myself, Thisby's father; Snug, the joiner, you, the lion's part; and, I hope, here is a play fitted.

SNUG
Have you the lion's part written? Pray you, if it be, give it me,
55 for I am slow of study.

QUINCE
You may do it extempore, for it is nothing but roaring.

BOTTOM
Let me play the lion too. I will roar, that I will do any man's heart good to hear me. I will roar, that I will make the Duke say, "Let him roar again, let him roar again."

QUINCE
60 An you should do it too terribly, you would fright the Duchess and the ladies, that they would shriek; and that were enough to hang us all.

ALL
That would hang us, every mother's son.

BOTTOM
I grant you, friends, if you should fright the ladies out of their
65 wits, they would have no more discretion but to hang us; but I will aggravate my voice so that I will roar you as gently as any sucking dove; I will roar you an 'twere any nightingale.

---

50 *tinker* a craftsman who repairs pots and pans. 52 *joiner* a craftsman who does woodwork. 66 *aggravate* Bottom really means "moderate."

BOTTOM
Well, go ahead.

QUINCE
Robin Starveling, the tailor.

STARVELING
Here, Peter Quince.

QUINCE
Robin Starveling, you must play Thisby's mother. Tom Snout,
50 the tinker.

SNOUT
Here, Peter Quince.

QUINCE
You will play Pyramus' father. I will play Thisby's father.
Snug, the joiner,
you will play the lion's part. I hope we have a well-cast play.

SNUG
Have you written down the lion's part? I beg you, if you
have, give it to me,
55 for I'm a slow study.

QUINCE
You may do it extemporaneously, for it's nothing but roaring.

BOTTOM
Let me play the lion, too. I will roar so that it will do any man's
heart good to hear me. I will roar so that I will make the duke say,
"Let him roar again, let him roar again."

QUINCE
60 If you did it too frighteningly, you would scare the duchess
and the ladies so that they would scream, and that'd be enough to
hang us all.

ALL
That would hang us, every mother's son of us.

BOTTOM
I'll admit, friends, that if the ladies would be frightened out of their
65 wits, they would have no more sense than to hang us, but I
will aggravate my voice so that I will roar as gently as any
sucking dove. I will roar as if I were a nightingale.

QUINCE

You can play no part but Pyramus; for Pyramus is a sweet-fac'd man; a proper man, as one shall see in a summer's day; a most
70 lovely gentleman-like man: therefore you must needs play Pyramus.

BOTTOM

Well, I will undertake it. What beard were I best to play it in?

QUINCE

Why, what you will.

BOTTOM

I will discharge it in either your straw-colour beard, your orange-
75 tawny beard, your purple-in-grain beard, or your French-crown-colour beard, your perfect yellow.

QUINCE

Some of your French crowns have no hair at all, and then you will play barefac'd. But, masters, here are your parts; and I am to entreat you, request you, and desire you, to con them by
80 tomorrow night; and meet me in the palace wood, a mile without the town, by moonlight. There will we rehearse, for if we meet in the city, we shall be dogg'd with company, and our devices known. In the meantime I will draw a bill of properties, such as our play wants. I pray you, fail me not.

BOTTOM

85 We will meet; and there we may rehearse most obscenely and courageously. Take pains; be perfect; adieu.

QUINCE

At the Duke's oak we meet.

BOTTOM

Enough; hold or cut bow-strings.

[*Exeunt.*]

---

75 *crown* means both "French coin" and "head." 77 *Some . . . hair* syphilis, which caused baldness, was supposed to be very common among the French. 85 *obscenely* another malapropism. Bottom probably means "in private." 88 *Hold . . . bow-strings* an archer's phrase.

QUINCE

You can play no part except Pyramus, for Pyramus is a sweet-faced man, as handsome a man as one shall see in a summer's day,
a most
70 lovely, gentlemanlike man. Therefore, you must play Pyramus.

BOTTOM

Well, I'll act the part. Which beard would it be best to play it in?

QUINCE

Why, do whatever you like.

BOTTOM

I will play the part in either your straw-colored beard, your orange-
75 tawny beard, your permanently dyed purple beard, or your
French gold-coin-
colored beard—your golden.

QUINCE

Some of your French crowns have no hair at all, so you would have to play it barefaced. But, gentlemen, here
are your parts. I
beg you, request you, and desire you to study them by
80 tomorrow night. And meet in the palace woods, a mile outside of town, by moonlight. There we'll rehearse, because if we meet in the city, we will be dogged by onlookers and our plans will be known. In the meantime, I will draw up a list of
props that we need for
our play. I beg you, don't fail me.

BOTTOM

85 We will meet, and there we'll rehearse most obscenely and courageously. Study hard, be perfect (in your parts). Goodbye.

QUINCE

We'll meet at the duke's oak.

BOTTOM

Good enough. Keep your word, or give up your parts.

They exit.

Act II, Scene i: [*A wood near Athens.*] *Enter a* FAIRY *at one door and* ROBIN GOODFELLOW *at another.*

ROBIN GOODFELLOW
How now, spirit! whither wander you?

FAIRY
Over hill, over dale,
Thorough bush, thorough brier,
Over park, over pale,
5 Thorough flood, thorough fire,
I do wander every where,
Swifter than the moon's sphere;
And I serve the fairy Queen,
To dew her orbs upon the green.
10 The cowslips tall her pensioners be;
In their gold coats spots you see;
Those be rubies, fairy favours,
In those freckles live their savours.
I must go seek some dewdrops here
15 And hang a pearl in every cowslips's ear.
Farewell, thou lob of spirits; I'll be gone.
Our Queen and all her elves come here anon.

ROBIN GOODFELLOW
The King doth keep his revels here tonight;
Take heed the Queen come not within his sight;
20 For Oberon is passing fell and wrath,
Because that she as her attendant hath
A lovely boy stolen from an Indian king.
She never had so sweet a changeling;
And jealous Oberon would have the child
25 Knight of his train, to trace the forests wild;
But she perforce withholds the loved boy,
Crowns him with flowers, and makes him all her joy;
And now they never meet in a grove or green,
By fountain clear, or spangled starlight sheen,
30 But they do square, that all their elves for fear
Creep into acorn-cups and hide them there.

---

10 *pensioners* Queen Elizabeth I's fifty noble bodyguards were called gentlemen pensioners. 23 *changeling* a child stolen by the fairies or the child they leave in the place of the kidnapped victim.

Act II, Scene i: A woods near Athens. Enter a fairy at one entrance and ROBIN GOODFELLOW, (PUCK), *at another.*

PUCK

Well, spirit, where are you wandering to?

FAIRY

Over hill, over dale,
Through bushes, through briers,
Over park, over land,
5 Through flood, through fire;
I wander everywhere
Swifter than the moon revolves.
I serve the fairy queen,
Putting dew on her fairy rings on the green.
10 The tall cowslips are her guards.
You can see spots on their gold coats,
Which are rubies, fairy gifts—
In those freckles is their perfumes.
I must go find some dewdrops here,
15 And hang a pearl in every cowslip's ear.
Goodbye, you clumsy lout of spirits. I'll go.
Our queen and all her elves will be here soon.

PUCK

King Oberon will hold his festivities here tonight.
Make sure the queen does not come near him
20 because Oberon is very enraged and angry
because she has taken for her attendant
a lovely boy whom she stole from an Indian king.
She never had such a sweet changeling.
Jealous Oberon wants the child to be
25 a knight in his train of followers who roam the wild forests.
But she withholds the beloved boy by force,
crowning him with flowers, and takes all her joy in him.
And now they (the king and queen) never meet in grove or green,
by clear fountain, or bright, shining starlight,
30 that they don't quarrel so that all their elves, out of fear,
crawl into acorn cups and hide there.

FAIRY

Either I mistake your shape and making quite,
Or else you are that shrewd and knavish sprite
Call'd Robin Goodfellow. Are not you he
35 That frights the maidens of the villagery,
Skim milk, and sometimes labour in the quern,
And bootless make the breathless housewife churn,
And sometime make the drink to bear no barm,
Mislead night-wanderers, laughing at their harm?
40 Those that Hobgoblin call you, and sweet Puck,
You do their work, and they shall have good luck.
Are not you he?

ROBIN GOODFELLOW

Thou speakest aright;
I am that merry wanderer of the night.
45 I jest to Oberon and make him smile
When I a fat and bean-fed horse beguile,
Neighing in likeness of a filly foal;
And sometime lurk I in a gossip's bowl,
In very likeness of a roasted crab,
50 And when she drinks, against her lips I bob
And on her withered dewlap pour the ale.
The wisest aunt, telling the saddest tale,
Sometime for three-foot stool mistaketh me.
Then slip I from her bum, down topples she,
55 And "tailor" cries, and falls into a cough;
And then the whole quire hold their hips and laugh,
And waxen in their mirth, and neeze, and swear
A merrier hour was never wasted there.
But, room, fairy! here comes Oberon.

FAIRY

60 And here my mistress. Would that he were gone!

Enter the King of Fairies, OBERON, *at one door with his train; and the Queen,* TITANIA, *at another with hers.*

OBERON

Ill met by moonlight, proud Titania.

---

40 *Puck* type of mischief-making hobgoblin. 49 *crab* or crab apples were frequently added to punches. 55 *tailor* the meaning is uncertain.

FAIRY

Either I mistake your shape and looks,
or you are that impish and mischievous elf
called Robin Goodfellow. Aren't you the one
35 who frightens the girls of the village folk,
skims the milk, and sometimes clogs the grain grinder?
Aren't you the one who makes the breathless housewife
churn for butter in vain?
And sometimes don't you make beer without yeast?
Don't you mislead night wanderers and laugh at the
scrapes they get into?
40 For those who call you Hobgoblin and sweet Puck,
you do their work, and they have good luck.
Aren't you the one (I've been talking about)?

PUCK

You are right.
I am that merry nighttime wanderer.
45 I make jokes for Oberon. I make him smile,
when I charm a fat and bean-fed horse
by neighing like a young filly.
And sometimes I lurk in an old woman's hot punch,
looking just like a roasted crab apple.
50 Then when she drinks, I bob against her lips,
and I pour ale on the withered skin of her throat.
The wisest old woman, telling the most serious story,
sometimes thinks I'm a three-foot stool.
Then I slip out from under her bum and she falls down,
55 and she cries "tailor" and starts to cough.
Then the whole group hold their hips and laugh,
and become merrier and sneeze and swear they
have never passed a happier hour there.
But, make way, fairy! Here comes Oberon.

FAIRY

60 And here comes my mistress. I wish he were gone.

Enter OBERON, *the king of Fairies, at one entrance with his train of followers, and* TITANIA, *the queen, at another with her followers.*

OBERON

This is an unwelcome meeting by moonlight, proud Titania.

TITANIA

What, jealous Oberon! Fairies, skip hence:
I have forsworn his bed and company.

OBERON

Tarry, rash wanton! Am not I thy lord?

TITANIA

65 Then I must be thy lady; but I know
When thou hast stolen away from fairy land,
And in the shape of Corin sat all day,
Playing on pipes of corn and versing love
To amorous Phillida. Why art thou here,
70 Come from the farthest steep of India?
But that, forsooth, the bouncing Amazon,
Your buskin'd mistress and your warrior love,
To Theseus must be wedded, and you come
To give their bed joy and prosperity.

OBERON

75 How canst thou thus for shame, Titania,
Glance at my credit with Hippolyta,
Knowing I know thy love to Theseus?
Didst thou not lead him through the glimmering night
From Perigenia, whom he ravished?
80 And make him with fair Aegle break his faith,
With Ariadne, and Antiopa?

TITANIA

These are the forgeries of jealousy;
And never, since the middle summer's spring,
Met we on hill, in dale, forest or mead,
85 By paved fountain or by rushy brook,
Or in the beached margent of the sea,
To dance our ringlets to the whistling wind,
But with thy brawls thou hast disturb'd our sport.
Therefore the winds, piping to us in vain,
90 As in revenge, have suck'd up from the sea
Contagious fogs; which, falling in the land,
Hath every pelting river made so proud

---

67 *Corin* like Phillida, a commonplace name for a lover in pastoral poetry. 72 *buskin'd* wearing high boots. 79-81 *Perigenia . . . Antiopa* Theseus' deserted lovers. Antiopa is usually considered to be another name for Hippolyta, but here, two different women are meant.

TITANIA

So! Jealous Oberon! Fairies, let's skip away.
I have vowed to avoid his bed and his company.

OBERON

Wait, rash, undisciplined woman! Am I not your lord?

TITANIA

65 Then I must be your lady. But I know
that you have skipped away from fairy land
and disguised as Corin sat all day
playing on grain stalk pipes and spouting love poetry
to the amorous Phillida. Why did you come here
70 from the most remote plain of India,
unless, of course, the swaggering Amazon,
your booted mistress and your warrior lover,
is going to be married to Theseus and you have come
to wish the couple joy and prosperity?

OBERON

75 For shame, Titania.
How can you slander my reputation with talk about Hippolyta,
when you know I know of your love for Theseus?
Didn't you lead him through the glimmering night
from Perigenia, whom he raped?
80 And then you made him break his promise to the lovely Aegle
and Ariadne and Antiopa?

TITANIA

Those are lies of jealousy.
Never, since the beginning of midsummer,
have we met on hill, in dale, forest, or meadow,
85 by pebble-bottomed fountain or by rush-lined brook,
or along the seashore,
to dance our circling steps in the whistling wind,
that you haven't disturbed our pleasure with your storms.
Therefore the winds whistle to us in vain,
90 as if out of revenge, having sucked up from the sea
fogs that carry disease, which, rolling inland,
have made every little river so proud

That they have overborne their continents.
The ox hath therefore stretch'd his yoke in vain,
95 The ploughman lost his sweat, and the green corn
Hath rotted ere his youth attain'd a beard.
The fold stands empty in the drowned field,
And crows are fatted with the murrain flock,
The nine men's morris is fill'd up with mud,
100 And the quaint mazes in the wanton green
For lack of tread are undistinguishable.
The human mortals want their winter cheer;
No night is now with hymn or carol blest.
Therefore the moon, the governess of floods,
105 Pale in her anger, washes all the air,
That rheumatic diseases do abound.
And thorough this distemperature we see
The seasons alter: hoary-headed frosts
Fall in the fresh lap of the crimson rose,
110 And on old Hiems' thin and icy crown
An odorous chaplet of sweet summer buds
Is, as in mockery, set; the spring, the summer,
The childing autumn, angry winter, change
Their wonted liveries; and the mazed world,
115 By their increase, now knows not which is which.
And this same progeny of evils comes
From our debate, from our dissension;
We are their parents and original.

OBERON

Do you amend it then; it lies in you.
120 Why should Titania cross her Oberon?
I do but beg a little changeling boy
To be my henchman.

TITANIA

Set your heart at rest;
The fairy land buys not the child of me.
125 His mother was a vot'ress of my order,
And, in the spiced Indian air, by night,
Full often hath she gossip'd by my side,

---

99 *nine men's morris* the squares created on a lawn for a checker-like game played outdoors. 110 *Hiem* the personification of winter.

that they have overflowed their banks.
Therefore the ox has pulled the plough in vain,
95 the plowman has wasted his sweat, and the green grain
has rotted before it could mature.
The pens stand empty in the drowned field,
and crows have grown fat on the dead diseased cattle.
The morris game field is full of mud,
100 and the intricate paths through the deep grass
have faded for lack of use.
The human mortals lack their winter cheer.
But no night is now made merry with a hymn or carol.
Therefore, the moon, the ruler of floods,
105 pale in her anger, washes all the air,
which is full of rheumatic diseases.
Through this disturbance in nature, we see
the seasons have been mixed up. White frosts
fall in the fresh lap of the crimson rose.
110 On old winter's thin and icy head,
a fragrant wreath of sweet summer buds
is placed in mockery. The spring, the summer,
the fruitful autumn, and angry winter change
their usual clothes, and the confused world
115 cannot tell which is which from nature's signs.
These very children of evil come
from our quarrel and from our argument.
We are their parents and origin.

OBERON
You had better correct it, then. It is up to you.
120 Why should Titania thwart her Oberon?
All I ask for is a little changeling boy
to be my page.

TITANIA
Set your heart at rest.
You could not buy him from me if you offered your entire
fairyland.
125 His mother was a woman who took a vow to worship me.
And in the spiced Indian air, at night,
she often chatted by my side

And sat with me on Neptune's yellow sands,
Marking th' embarked traders on the flood,
130 When we have laugh'd to see the sails conceive
And grow big-bellied with the wanton wind;
Which she with pretty and with swimming gait
Following, her womb then rich with my young squire,
Would imitate, and sail upon the land
135 To fetch me trifles, and return again,
As from a voyage, rich with merchandise.
But she, being mortal, of that boy did die;
And for her sake do I rear up her boy,
And for her sake I will not part with him.

OBERON
140 How long within this wood intend you stay?

TITANIA
Perchance till after Theseus' wedding-day.
If you will patiently dance in our round
And see our moonlight revels, go with us;
If not, shun me, and I will spare your haunts.

OBERON
145 Give me that boy, and I will go with thee.

TITANIA
Not for thy fairy kingdom. Fairies, away!
We shall chide downright, if I longer stay.
[*Exit* TITANIA *with her train.*]

OBERON
Well, go thy way; thou shalt not from this grove
Till I torment thee for this injury.
150 My gentle Puck, come hither. Thou rememb'rest
Since once I sat upon a promontory,
And heard a mermaid on a dolphin's back
Uttering such dulcet and harmonious breath
That the rude sea grew civil at her song,
155 And certain stars shot madly from their spheres,
To hear the sea-maid's music?

---

128 *Neptune* the god who ruled the ocean.

and sat with me on the sea's yellow sands.
We watched the sailing traders on the sea
130 and laughed to see the sails conceive
and grow fat with the playful winds.
She, with a pretty and graceful walk—
her womb then was filled with my young page—
would imitate the ship and sail across the land
135 to fetch me little things and return again—
as if from a voyage—rich with merchandise.
But she, being just a mortal, died delivering the boy.
For her sake, I raise her boy,
and for her sake, I will not part with him.

OBERON
140 How long do you intend to stay in this woods?

TITANIA
Perhaps until after Theseus' wedding day.
If you will patiently join in our circular dance
and see our moonlight festivities, come with us.
If not, avoid me, and I will keep away from you.

OBERON
145 Give me that boy, and I'll go with you.

TITANIA
Not for your fairy kingdom. Fairies, let's be off!
We will quarrel outright if I stay any longer.
Exit TITANIA *and her train.*

OBERON
Well, go on your way. But, you will not leave this woods
until I punish you for this insult.
150 My gentle Puck, come here. You remember
the time I once sat on a promontory
and heard a mermaid, on a dolphin's back,
singing such sweet and harmonious notes
that the rude sea grew well-behaved when she sang,
155 and some stars shot madly out of their orbits
to hear the sea maiden's music.

ROBIN GOODFELLOW
I remember.

OBERON
That very time I saw, but thou couldst not,
Flying between the cold moon and the earth,
160 Cupid all arm'd. A certain aim he took
At a fair vestal throned by the west,
And loos'd his love-shaft smartly from his bow,
As it should pierce a hundred thousand hearts;
But I might see young Cupid's fiery shaft
165 Quench'd in the chaste beams of the wat'ry moon,
And the imperial vot'ress passed on,
In maiden meditation, fancy-free.
Yet mark'd I where the bolt of Cupid fell.
It fell upon a little western flower,
170 Before milk-white, now purple with love's wound,
And maidens call it love-in-idleness.
Fetch me that flower, the herb I shew'd thee once.
The juice of it on sleeping eye-lids laid
Will make or man or woman madly dote
175 Upon the next live creature that it sees.
Fetch me this herb; and be thou here again
Ere the leviathan can swim a league.

ROBIN GOODFELLOW
I'll put a girdle round about the earth
In forty minutes.
[*Exit.*]

OBERON
180 Having once this juice,
I'll watch Titania when she is asleep,
And drop the liquor of it in her eyes.
The next thing then she waking looks upon,
Be it on lion, bear, or wolf, or bull,
185 On meddling monkey, or on busy ape,
She shall pursue it with the soul of love;
And ere I take this charm from off her sight,
As I can take it with another herb,

---

161 *vestal* usually considered to be a reference to Queen Elizabeth I. (The queen may have been present when *A Midsummer Night's Dream* was first performed.) 171 *love-in-idleness* another name for the flower, the pansy.

PUCK

I remember.

OBERON

On that particular occasion I saw (but you could not),
flying between the cold moon and the earth,
160 Cupid, all armed with arrows. He took aim
at a lovely virgin enthroned by the west,
and he shot his love arrow briskly from his bow,
as if he meant it to pierce a hundred thousand hearts.
But I could see young Cupid's fiery arrow
165 quenched in the pure beams of the watery moon,
and the regal worshipper passed on
in virginal meditation, free from the influence of love.
Yet I saw where Cupid's arrow fell.
It fell upon a little western flower,
170 that was once milk-white and now is purple from love's wound.
Girls call it "love-in-idleness."
Bring me that flower; I showed it to you once.
If the juice of it is dropped on sleeping eyelids,
it will make either man or woman adore
175 the next creature he or she sees.
Bring me this flower, and be back again
before the whale can swim three miles.

PUCK

I'll fly around the earth
in forty minutes.

He exits.

OBERON

180 Once I have this juice,
I'll wait until Titania is asleep
and drop this juice in her eyes.
When she awakes, the first thing she looks at,
whether it be a lion, a bear, a wolf, a bull,
185 a meddling monkey, or an annoying ape,
she will pursue it with all her love.
And before I lift this magical charm from her vision
(I can remove it with another herb),

I'll make her render up her page to me.
190 But who comes here? I am invisible;
And I will overhear their conference.

Enter DEMETRIUS, HELENA *following him.*

DEMETRIUS

I love thee not, therefore pursue me not.
Where is Lysander and fair Hermia?
The one I'll stay, the other stayeth me.
195 Thou told'st me they were stol'n unto this wood;
And here am I, and wood within this wood
Because I cannot meet my Hermia.
Hence, get thee gone, and follow me no more.

HELENA

You draw me, you hard-hearted adamant;
200 But yet you draw not iron, for my heart
Is true as steel. Leave you your power to draw,
And I shall have no power to follow you.

DEMETRIUS

Do I entice you? Do I speak you fair?
Or, rather, do I not in plainest truth
205 Tell you, I do not nor I cannot love you?

HELENA

And even for that do I love you the more.
I am your spaniel, and, Demetrius,
The more you beat me, I will fawn on you.
Use me but as your spaniel, spurn me, strike me,
210 Neglect me, lose me; only give me leave,
Unworthy as I am, to follow you.
What worser place can I beg in your love,—
And yet a place of high respect with me,—
Than to be used as you use your dog?

DEMETRIUS

215 Tempt not too much the hatred of my spirit,
For I am sick when I do look on thee.

HELENA

And I am sick when I look not on you.

---

199 *adamant* means both a magnet and a type of very hard metal. 200 *iron* another hard metal and metaphorically, therefore, unfeeling and cold.

I'll make her give up her page to me.
190 But who is coming? Since I'm invisible,
I will listen to their conversation.
Enter DEMETRIUS *with* HELENA *following him.*

DEMETRIUS
I don't love you, so stop following me.
Where is Lysander and the lovely Hermia?
One of them I'd like to kill; the other one is killing me.
195 You told me that they had sneaked off into this woods.
And here I am, out of my mind within this woods
because I cannot find my Hermia.
Go, be off, and don't follow me anymore!

HELENA
You draw me to you, you hardhearted magnet.
200 But you are not attracting iron because my heart
is as true as steel. Give up your power to attract,
and I will not have the power to follow you.

DEMETRIUS
Do I entice you? Do I speak to you kindly?
Or, rather, don't I tell you as bluntly as possible
205 that I do not and cannot love you?

HELENA
And even for that very reason I love you all the more.
I am your spaniel, and, Demetrius,
the more you beat me, the more I will fawn on you.
Treat me just like your spaniel—reject me, hit me,
210 neglect me, lose me—only, give me permission,
(unworthy as I am), to follow you.
What lower place can I beg for in your love—
(and yet it would be a wonderful place to me)
than to be treated as you would your dog?

DEMETRIUS
215 Don't tempt my hatred too much,
because I grow sick whenever I see you.

HELENA
And I grow sick whenever I cannot see you.

DEMETRIUS
You do impeach your modesty too much,
To leave the city and commit yourself
220 Into hands of one that loves you not;
To trust the opportunity of night
And the ill counsel of a desert place
With the rich worth of your virginity.

HELENA
Your virtue is my privilege. For that
225 It is not night when I do see your face,
Therefore I think I am not in the night;
Nor doth this wood lack worlds of company,
For you in my respect are all the world.
Then how can it be said I am alone,
230 When all the world is here to look on me?

DEMETRIUS
I'll run from thee and hide me in the brakes,
And leave thee to the mercy of wild beasts.

HELENA
The wildest hath not such a heart as you.
Run when you will, the story shall be chang'd:
235 Apollo flies, and Daphne holds the chase;
The dove pursues the griffin; the mild hind
Makes speed to catch the tiger: bootless speed,
When cowardice pursues and valour flies.

DEMETRIUS
I will not stay thy questions; let me go;
240 Or, if thou follow me, do not believe
But I shall do thee mischief in the wood.

HELENA
Ay, in the temple, in the town, the field,
You do me mischief. Fie, Demetrius!
Your wrongs do set a scandal on my sex.
245 We cannot fight for love, as men may do.
We should be woo'd and were not made to woo.
[*Exit* DEMETRIUS.]

---

235 *Apollo . . . Daphne* the Greek god Apollo chased the nymph Daphne until she turned into a tree. 236 *griffin* a mythical beast with a lion's body and the head, wings, and front feet of a bird.

DEMETRIUS

You're damaging your reputation too much
by leaving the city and putting yourself
220 into the hands of someone who doesn't love you.
You are trusting the dangerous possibilities of night
and the risky seclusion of a deserted place
with the rich value of your virtue.

HELENA

Your powerful appeal allows me to do so. Since
225 it is never night when I see your face,
I never think it is night.
Nor is this woods lacking for plenty of company,
because you, in my opinion, are the entire world.
So how can it be said I am alone
230 when all the world is here to see me?

DEMETRIUS

I'll run from you and hide in the thickets,
and leave you to the mercy of the wild animals.

HELENA

The wildest beast doesn't have a heart like yours.
Run when you wish—I'll change the old story:
235 Apollo runs, and Daphne chases him;
the dove pursues the griffin; the gentle doe
hurries to catch the tiger—useless speed
when a coward chases and the brave runs!

DEMETRIUS

I won't wait to listen to you. Let me go!
240 If you follow me, believe me,
I'll see that you come to some harm in the woods.

HELENA

Yes, in the temple, in the town, in the field,
you hurt me. Shame on you, Demetrius!
The wrongs you have done to me have made a scandal of my
womanhood.
245 Women cannot fight for love as men may do.
Women have to be pursued. We were not made to pursue.

Exit DEMETRIUS.

I'll follow thee and make a heaven of hell,
To die upon the hand I love so well.
[*Exit.*]

OBERON
Fare thee well, nymph. Ere he do leave this grove,
250 Thou shalt fly him and he shall seek thy love.
Re-enter ROBIN GOODFELLOW.
Has thou the flower there? Welcome, wanderer.

ROBIN GOODFELLOW
Ay, there it is.

OBERON
I pray thee, give it me.
I know a bank where the wild thyme blows,
255 Where oxlips and the nodding violet grows,
Quite over-canopi'd with luscious woodbine,
With sweet musk-roses and with eglantine.
There sleeps Titania sometime of the night,
Lull'd in these flowers with dances and delight;
260 And there the snake throws her enamell'd skin,
Weed wide enough to wrap a fairy in;
And with the juice of this I'll streak her eyes,
And make her full of hateful fantasies.
Take thou some of it, and seek through this grove.
265 A sweet Athenian lady is in love
With a disdainful youth. Anoint his eyes,
But do it when the next thing he espies
May be the lady. Thou shalt know the man
By the Athenian garments he hath on.
270 Effect it with some care, that he may prove
More fond on her than she upon her love;
And look thou meet me ere the first cock crow.

ROBIN GOODFELLOW
Fear not, my lord, your servant shall do so.
[*Exeunt.*]

I'll follow you and make a heaven out of hell.
I'll die by your hand which I love so well.
She exits.

OBERON
Goodbye, nymph. Before he leaves this wood,
250 you shall run from him, and he will seek your love.
Enter PUCK.
Do you have the flower there? Welcome wanderer.

PUCK
Yes, there it is.

OBERON
Please give it to me.
I know a bank where the wild thyme blows,
255 where oxlips and the nodding violet grows,
all covered with luscious woodbine,
sweet musk roses, and eglantine.
Sometime Titania sleeps there at night,
lulled to sleep in these flowers with wonderful dances.
260 And there the snake sheds her enameled skin,
a garment wide enough to wrap a fairy in.
And with the juice of this flower, I'll streak her eyes,
and fill her full of hateful delusions.
Take some of this juice, and look through these woods.
265 A sweet Athenian lady is in love
with a scornful youth. Pour the flower juice in his eyes,
but do it so that the next thing he sees
will be this lady. You will recognize the man
by the Athenian clothes he has on.
270 Be sure to do this carefully so that he will become
more foolishly in love with her than she is with him.
And be sure to meet me before the first rooster crows.

PUCK
Don't worry, my lord, I will do so.
They exit.

Act II, Scene ii: [*Another part of the wood.*] *Enter* TITANIA, *with her train.*

TITANIA

Come, now a roundel and a fairy song;
Then, for the third part of a minute, hence,
Some to kill cankers in the musk-rose buds,
Some war with rere-mice for their leathern wings
5 To make my small elves coats, and some keep back
The clamorous owl that nightly hoots and wonders
At our quaint spirits. Sing me now asleep;
Then to your offices and let me rest.
[THE FAIRIES *sing.*]

1. FAIRY

"You spotted snakes with double tongue,
10 Thorny hedgehogs, be not seen;
Newts and blind-worms, do no wrong,
Come not near our fairy queen."

CHORUS

"Philomel, with melody
Sing in our sweet lullaby;
15 Lulla, lulla, lullaby; lulla, lulla, lullaby.
Never harm
Nor spell nor charm
Come our lovely lady nigh.
So, good night, with lullaby."

1. FAIRY

20 "Weaving spiders, come not here;
Hence, you long-legg'd spinners, hence!
Beatles black, approach not near;
Worm nor snail, do no offence."

CHORUS

"Philomel, with melody," etc.

2. FAIRY

25 Hence, away! now all is well.
One aloof stand sentinel.
[*Exeunt* FAIRIES. TITANIA *sleeps.*]

---

13 *Philomel* name for the nightingale taken from the Greek girl Philomel who was changed into a nightingale.

Act II, Scene ii: Another part of the woods. Enter TITANIA *with her followers.*

TITANIA

Come! Now dance in a ring and sing a fairy song.
Then for a third of a minute, leave here.
Some of you shall go to kill cankerworms in the musk rose buds,
some to fight bats for their leather wings
5 to make coats for my small elves, and some to chase away
the noisy owl that nightly hoots and wonders
at our dainty spirits. Sing me to sleep now.
Then do your duties, and let me sleep.

(The fairies sing.)

FIRST FAIRY

You spotted snakes with double tongues,
10 And thorny hedgehogs, stay away.
Newts and little snakes, do no wrong.
Don't come near our fairy queen.

CHORUS

Philomel, with melody
Join our sweet lullaby.
15 Lulla, lulla, lullaby, lulla, lulla, lullaby,
No harm
Or spell, or charm,
Must come near our lovely lady.
So, good night, with lullaby.

FIRST FAIRY

20 Weaving spiders, don't come here.
Away, you long-legged spinners of webs, away!
Black beetles, do not approach.
Worms and snails, do no harm.

CHORUS

Nightingale, with melody (repeat chorus).

SECOND FAIRY

25 Away, away! Now all is well.
One of you keep watch over her from a distance.

The fairies exit. TITANIA *sleeps.*

Enter OBERON *and squeezes the flower on* TITANIA'S *eyelids.*

OBERON

What thou seest when thou dost wake,
Do it for thy true-love take,
Love and languish for his sake.
30 Be it ounce, or cat, or bear,
Pard, or boar with bristled hair,
In thy eye that shall appear
When thou wak'st, it is thy dear.
Wake when some vile thing is near.
[*Exit.*]

Enter LYSANDER *and* HERMIA.

LYSANDER

35 Fair love, you faint with wand'ring in the wood;
And to speak troth, I have forgot our way.
We'll rest us, Hermia, if you think it good,
And tarry for the comfort of the day.

HERMIA

Be it so, Lysander. Find you out a bed;
40 For I upon this bank will rest my head.

LYSANDER

One turf shall serve as pillow for us both;
One heart, one bed, two bosoms and one troth.

HERMIA

Nay, good Lysander; for my sake, my dear,
Lie further off yet; do not lie so near.

LYSANDER

45 O, take the sense, sweet, of my innocence!
Love takes the meaning in love's conference.
I mean, that my heart unto yours is knit
So that but one heart we can make of it;
Two bosoms interchained with an oath,
50 So then two bosoms and a single troth.
Then by your side no bed-room me deny;
For lying so, Hermia, I do not lie.

OBERON *enters and squeezes the flower's juice on* TITANIA'S *eyelids.*

OBERON

The first thing you see when you awake,
You will choose for your true love.
You will love and long for him,
30 Whether it be a lynx, a wildcat, or a bear,
A leopard, or a hog with bristled hair.
Whatever meets your eye
When you awake, it will be your beloved.
Awake when some repulsive thing is near.

He exits.

Enter LYSANDER *and* HERMIA.

LYSANDER

35 My beautiful love, you are weak from wandering in the woods.
And to tell the truth, I have forgotten which way to go.
Let us rest, Hermia, if you agree,
and wait for the comfort of daylight.

HERMIA

Let us do that, Lysander. Find a bed.
40 Upon this bank, I will rest my head.

LYSANDER

One piece of ground will serve as a bed for us both;
one heart, one bed, two bosoms, and one vow of love.

HERMIA

No, good Lysander. For my sake, my dear,
lie farther off. Do not lie so close.

LYSANDER

45 Please understand what I said in innocence, my sweet.
Lovers understand each other's real meaning when they speak.
I mean that my heart is joined with yours
so that together we have just one heart.
Our two bosoms are chained together with a vow,
50 so we have two bosoms and one single love.
So don't refuse to allow me to sleep by your side.
For lying there beside you, Hermia, I would not be untrue.

HERMIA

Lysander riddles very prettily.
Now much beshrew my manners and my pride,
55 If Hermia meant to say Lysander lied.
But, gentle friend, for love and courtesy
Lie further off; in humane modesty,
Such separation as may well be said
Becomes a virtuous bachelor and a maid,
60 So far be distant; and, good night, sweet friend.
Thy love ne'er alter till thy sweet life end!

LYSANDER

Amen, amen, to that fair prayer, say I;
And then end life when I end loyalty!
Here is my bed; sleep give thee all his rest!

HERMIA

65 With half that wish the wisher's eyes be press'd!
[*They sleep.*]

Enter ROBIN GOODFELLOW.

ROBIN GOODFELLOW

Through the forest have I gone,
But Athenian found I none,
On whose eyes I might approve
This flower's force in stirring love.
70 Night and silence—Who is here?
Weeds of Athens he doth wear!
This is he, my master said,
Despised the Athenian maid;
And here the maiden, sleeping sound,
75 On the dank and dirty ground.
Pretty soul! she durst not lie
Near this lack-love, this kill-courtesy.
Churl, upon thy eyes I throw
All the power this charm doth owe.

---

54 *beshrew* means curse but usually is not intended to be taken very gravely.

HERMIA

Lysander, you make very nice riddles.
Now my manners and my pride should really be much cursed
55 if I meant to imply that you lied.
But, gentle friend, out of love and courtesy,
lie farther away, for the sake of human modesty.
It could well be said that such separation
is proper for a virtuous bachelor and a girl.
60 So keep your distance, and good night, sweet friend.
Never change your love as long as you live!

LYSANDER

Amen, amen, to that beautiful prayer I sing.
And may I die when I'm no longer loyal to you.
Here is my bed over here. May sleep give you all his rest.

HERMIA

65 I wish that half that wish may be pressed on the eyes
of the wisher!

(They go to sleep.)

Enter PUCK.

PUCK

I have gone through the forest,
But I found no Athenian
On whose eyes I could test
This flower's power to cause love.
70 Night and silence! Who is this here?
He is wearing Athenian clothes.
This is the man who my master said
Despised the Athenian maiden.
And here is the maiden, sleeping soundly
75 On the damp and dirty ground.
She is a pretty soul. She does not dare lie
Near this man who doesn't love her, this rude man.
Rascal, upon your eyes I throw
All the power this charm possesses.

80 When thou wak'st, let love forbid
Sleep his seat on thy eyelid;
So awake when I am gone,
For I must now to Oberon.
[*Exit.*]

Enter DEMETRIUS *and* HELENA, *running.*

HELENA
Stay, though thou kill me, sweet Demetrius.

DEMETRIUS
85 I charge thee, hence, and do not haunt me thus.

HELENA
O, wilt thou darkling leave me? Do not so.

DEMETRIUS
Stay, on thy peril; I alone will go.
[*Exit.*]

HELENA
O, I am out of breath in this fond chase!
The more my prayer, the lesser is my grace.
90 Happy is Hermia, wheresoe'er she lies,
For she hath blessed and attractive eyes.
How came her eyes so bright? Not with salt tears;
If so, my eyes are oft'ner wash'd than hers.
No, no, I am as ugly as a bear,
95 For beasts that meet me run away for fear;
Therefore no marvel though Demetrius
Do, as a monster, fly my presence thus.
What wicked and dissembling glass of mine
Made me compare with Hermia's sphery eyne?
100 But who is here? Lysander! on the ground!
Dead? or asleep? I see no blood, no wound.
Lysander, if you live, good sir, awake.

LYSANDER
[*Awaking.*] And run through fire I will for thy
sweet sake.

80 When you awake, let love keep
Sleep from resting on your eyelids.
So awake when I have left,
For I must now go to Oberon.
He exits.
Enter DEMETRIUS *and* HELENA, *running.*

HELENA
Wait, if you must kill me, sweet Demetrius.

DEMETRIUS
85 I order you, leave, and do not chase after me like this.

HELENA
O, will you leave me in the dark? Do not do that.

DEMETRIUS
Stay here, I'm warning you! I will go alone.
He exits.

HELENA
O, I am out of breath from this foolish chase.
The more I beg, the less I am forgiven.
90 Hermia is happy, wherever she lies,
because she has blessed and attractive eyes.
How did her eyes get to be so bright? Not from salty tears.
If that's the reason, my eyes are washed (with tears) more
often than hers.
No, no! I am as ugly as a bear,
95 because beasts that see me run away out of fear.
Therefore, it is no wonder that Demetrius
runs away from me as though I were a monster.
What wicked and lying mirror
made me compare my eyes with Hermia's starry eyes?
100 But who is this? Lysander! Here on the ground.
Is he dead? or asleep? I see no blood, no wound.
Lysander, if you are alive, good sir, wake up.

LYSANDER *(Awakening)*
And I will run through fire for your sweet sake.

Transparent Helena! Nature shows art,
105 That through thy bosom makes me see thy heart.
Where is Demetrius? O, how fit a word
Is that vile name to perish on my sword!

HELENA
Do not say so, Lysander; say not so.
What though he love your Hermia? Lord, what though?
110 Yet Hermia still loves you; then be content.

LYSANDER
Content with Hermia! No; I do repent
The tedious minutes I with her have spent.
Not Hermia but Helena I love.
Who will not change a raven for a dove?
115 The will of man is by his reason sway'd;
And reason says you are the worthier maid.
Things growing are not ripe until their season,
So I, being young, till now ripe not to reason;
And touching now the point of human skill,
120 Reason becomes the marshal to my will
And leads me to your eyes, where I o'erlook
Love's stories written in Love's richest book.

HELENA
Wherefore was I to this keen mockery born?
When at your hands did I deserve this scorn?
125 Is't not enough, is't not enough, young man,
That I did never, no, nor never can,
Deserve a sweet look from Demetrius' eye,
But you must flout my insufficiency?
Good troth, you do me wrong, good sooth you do,
130 In such disdainful manner me to woo.
But fare you well; perforce I must confess
I thought you lord of more true gentleness.
O, that a lady, of one man refus'd,
Should of another therefore be abus'd!
[*Exit.*]

---

114 *raven for a dove* Lysander compares nature as well as the coloring of the blonde Helena and the darker Hermia.

Brilliantly beautiful Helena, nature instructs understanding
105 so that through your bosom, I can see your heart.
Where is Demetrius? O, how fitting it
would be for that disgusting name to die by my sword.

HELENA
Don't say that, Lysander; don't say that.
What does it matter that he loves your Hermia? Lord,
what does it matter?
110 Hermia still loves you, so be happy.

LYSANDER
Happy with Hermia? No. I repent
the tedious minutes I have spent with her.
It is not Hermia, but you, Helena, whom I love.
Who wouldn't trade a raven for a dove?
115 Man's desires are often swayed by his reason,
and my reason says you are the better woman.
Fruit does not ripen until it is ready.
So I, being young, have not had mature understandings until now.
But now that I have reached a maturity of human reason,
120 reason becomes the guide of my will,
and leads me to your eyes. There I see
love's stories, written in love's richest book.

HELENA
Why was I born to bear this biting mockery?
What did I do to deserve this scorn from you?
125 Isn't it enough, isn't it enough, young man,
that I never did—no, nor ever could—
deserve a sweet look from Demetrius' eyes,
but that you, too, make fun of my inadequacies?
Really, you do me wrong! Indeed you do
130 to speak of love to me in such a contemptible manner.
Goodbye. I must confess that
I thought you were a more honestly noble man.
It is too bad that a lady, refused by one man,
should therefore be abused by another.
She exits.

LYSANDER

135 She sees not Hermia. Hermia, sleep thou there;
And never mayst thou come Lysander near!
For as a surfeit of the sweetest things
The deepest loathing to the stomach brings,
Or as the heresies that men do leave
140 Are hated most of those they did deceive,
So thou, my surfeit and my heresy,
Of all be hated, but the most of me!
And, all my powers, address your love and might
To honour Helen and to be her knight.
[*Exit.*]

HERMIA

145 [*Awaking.*] Help me, Lysander, help me! do thy best
To pluck this crawling serpent from my breast!
Ay me, for pity! what a dream was here!
Lysander, look how I do quake with fear.
Methought a serpent eat my heart away,
150 And you sat smiling at his cruel prey.
Lysander! what, remov'd? Lysander! lord!
What, out of hearing? Gone? No sound, no word?
Alack, where are you? Speak, an if you hear;
Speak, of all loves! I swoon almost with fear.
155 No? then I well perceive you are not nigh.
Either death or you I'll find immediately.
[*Exit.*]

Act III, Scene i: [*The wood.* TITANIA *lying asleep.*] *Enter the Clowns* QUINCE, SNUG, BOTTOM, FLUTE, SNOUT, *and* STARVELING.

BOTTOM

Are we all met?

QUINCE

Pat, pat; and here's a marvellous convenient place for our rehearsal. This green plot shall be our stage, this hawthorn-brake our tiring-house; and we will do it in action as we will do it before
5 the Duke.

LYSANDER

135 She didn't see Hermia. Hermia, stay asleep over there,
and don't ever come near me.
Just as gorging on sweet things
makes you sick of the taste,
or as the heresies that men speak
140 are hated most by those they deceived,
so, you Hermia, are my gorging and my heresy,
hated by all, but most of all, by me!
Now, Lysander, use all your powers and use your love and strength
to honor Helen and be her knight!

He exits.

HERMIA *(Awakening)*

145 Help me, Lysander, help me! Please
pull this crawling snake from my breast!
O me, for pity's sake, what a dream I had!
Lysander, see how I'm shaking with fear.
I thought a snake ate my heart away,
150 and you sat smiling at his cruel act.
Lysander! What, are you gone? Lysander! Lord!
What, are you out of hearing? Gone? Not a sound, not a word?
Alas, where are you? Speak, if you can hear me.
Speak for love's sake. I am almost fainting with fear.
155 No? Then I can see you are not nearby.
I'll find either you or death immediately.

She exits.

Act III, Scene i: The woods. TITANIA *is lying asleep. Enter* QUINCE, SNUG, BOTTOM, FLUTE, SNOUT, *and* STARVELING.

BOTTOM

Are we all here?

QUINCE

Exactly, exactly. And here's a marvelously convenient place for us
to rehearse. This grassy spot will be our stage, this hawthorn thicket
our dressing room, and we'll perform just like we'll do it before
5 the duke.

BOTTOM
Peter Quince!

QUINCE
What say'st thou, bully Bottom?

BOTTOM
There are things in this comedy of Pyramus and Thisby that will never please. First, Pyramus must draw a sword to kill himself,
10 which the ladies cannot abide. How answer you that?

SNOUT
By'r lakin, a parlous fear.

STARVELING
I believe we must leave the killing out, when all is done.

BOTTOM
Not a whit! I have a device to make all well. Write me a prologue; and let the prologue seem to say, we will do no harm with our
15 swords and that Pyramus is not kill'd indeed; and, for the more better assurance, tell them that I Pyramus am not Pyramus, but Bottom the weaver. This will put them out of fear.

QUINCE
Well, we will have such a prologue; and it shall be written in eight and six.

BOTTOM
20 No, make it two more; let it be written in eight and eight.

SNOUT
Will not the ladies be afeard of the lion?

STARVELING
I fear it, I promise you.

BOTTOM
Masters, you ought to consider with yourselves. To bring in—God shield us!—a lion among ladies, is a most dreadful thing;
25 for there is not a more fearful wild-fowl than your lion living; and we ought to look to't.

SNOUT
Therefore another prologue must tell he is not a lion.

---

11 *lakin* a corruption of lady kin, or little lady. The Virgin Mary is being referred to.
18-19 *eight and six* ballads consist of alternating lines of eight and six syllables.

BOTTOM
Peter Quince!

QUINCE
What do you want, good fellow, Bottom?

BOTTOM
There are things in this comedy of Pyramus and Thisby that will
never be appealing. First, Pyramus must draw a sword to kill himself,
10 which the ladies would never like. What do you say about that?

SNOUT
By Our Lady, that is a terrible problem!

STARVELING
I think we'd better leave the killing out, after all.

BOTTOM
Not at all. I have a way to make everything turn out fine. Write me a prologue,
and let the prologue say that we will do no harm with our
15 swords, and that Pyramus is not really killed. To give them even more
reassurance, tell them that I, the one playing Pyramus, am not Pyramus but
Bottom the weaver. That will keep them from being afraid.

QUINCE
All right, we will have such a prologue, and it shall be in lines of eight
and six syllables.

BOTTOM
20 No, make it two more syllables. Let it be written in eight and eight syllables.

SNOUT
Won't the ladies be afraid of the lion?

STARVELING
I'm afraid they will, I swear.

BOTTOM
Masters, you should think this over. To bring in—
God help us!—a lion among ladies, is a most dreadful thing.
25 For there is not a more fearful wild fowl alive than a lion.
And we should do something about it.

SNOUT
Therefore, another prologue must say that he's not a lion.

BOTTOM

Nay, you must name his name, and half his face must be seen through the lion's neck; and he himself must speak through, 30 saying thus, or to the same defect, "Ladies," or "Fair ladies, I would wish you," or "I would request you," or "I would entreat you, not to fear, not to tremble: my life for yours. If you think I come hither as a lion, it were pity of my life. No, I am no such thing; I am a man as other men are;" and there indeed let him 35 name his name, and tell them plainly he is Snug the joiner.

QUINCE

Well, it shall be so. But there is two hard things; that is, to bring the moonlight into a chamber; for, you know, Pyramus and Thisby meet by moonlight.

SNOUT

Doth the moon shine that night we play our play?

BOTTOM

40 A calendar, a calendar! Look in the almanac! Find out moonshine, find out moonshine.

QUINCE

Yes, it doth shine that night.

BOTTOM

Why, then may you leave a casement of the great chamber window, where we play, open, and the moon may shine in at the 45 casement.

QUINCE

Ay; or else one must come in with a bush of thorns and a lantern, and say he comes to disfigure, or to present, the person of Moonshine. Then, there is another thing: we must have a wall in the great chamber; for Pyramus and Thisby, says the story, did talk 50 through the chink of a wall.

SNOUT

You can never bring in a wall. What say you, Bottom?

BOTTOM

Some man or other must present Wall; and let him have some plaster, or some loam, or some rough-cast about him, to signify

---

30 *defect* Bottom's malapropism for "effect." 46-48 *bush . . . Moonshine* according to some tales, the man in the moon was said to have been sentenced to live on the moon after sinning by collecting firewood on the holy day of Sunday.

BOTTOM

No, you must give his name, and half his face must be seen
through the lion's neck, and he himself must speak,
30 saying this—or something to the same defect: "Ladies,"
or "Lovely ladies, I
wish you," or "I request you," or "I beg
you, not to be afraid or tremble. I'd give my life for yours. If
you think
I come here as a lion, it would be my head on the block.
No! I'm no such
thing. I'm a man just like other men." And at that point, let him
35 give his name and tell them plainly that he is Snug the joiner.

QUINCE

Well, we'll do it like that. But there still are two problems. One is
how to make
the moonlight fall into the hall because, you know, Pyramus and
Thisby meet by moonlight.

SNOUT

Does the moon shine the night we play our play?

BOTTOM

40 A calendar, get a calendar! Look in the almanac. Find out if the moon
shines, find out if the moon shines!

QUINCE

Yes, it shines that night.

BOTTOM

Well, then you may leave a window open in the large hall
where we'll put on our play, and the moon will shine in through the
45 window.

QUINCE

Yes, or else one of us must come in with a bush of thorns
and a lantern
and say that he comes to disfigure or represent the character Moonshine. Then there is another thing. We must have a wall in the
great hall because Pyramus and Thisby talked
50 through a crack in the wall, according to the story.

SNOUT

You can never bring in a wall. What do you say, Bottom?

BOTTOM

Someone or other must pretend to be the wall. And he should
have some
plaster, or some soil, or some plaster and pebbles covering him,
to show that he is a

wall; or let him hold his fingers thus, and through that cranny
55 shall Pyramus and Thisby whisper.

QUINCE

If that may be, then all is well. Come, sit down, every mother's son, and rehearse your parts. Pyramus, you begin. When you have spoken your speech, enter into that brake. And so every one according to his cue.

Enter ROBIN GOODFELLOW *behind.*

ROBIN GOODFELLOW

60 What hempen home-spuns have we swagg'ring here,
So near the cradle of the fairy queen?
What, a play toward! I'll be an auditor;
An actor too perhaps, if I see cause.

QUINCE

Speak, Pyramus. Thisby, stand forth.

BOTTOM

65 "Thisby, the flowers of odious savours sweet,"—

QUINCE

Odorous, odorous.

BOTTOM

—"Odours savours sweet;
So hath thy breath, my dearest Thisby dear.
But hark, a voice! Stay thou but here awhile,
70 And by and by I will to thee appear."
[*Exit.*]

ROBIN GOODFELLOW

A stranger Pyramus than e'er play'd here.
[*Exit.*]

FLUTE

Must I speak now?

QUINCE

Ay, marry, must you; for you must understand he goes but to see a noise that he heard, and is to come again.

wall. And let him hold his fingers like this. Through that crack,
55 Pyramus and Thisby will whisper.

QUINCE
If we do that, all will be well. Come, sit down, every mother's son of you. Rehearse your parts. Pyramus, you begin. When you have
delivered your speech, go into that thicket. Everyone else do the scene according to your cue.
Enter PUCK.

PUCK
60 What kind of crude yokels do we have swaggering here,
so near the bed of the fairy queen?
What's this? A play about to begin? I'll be a listener—
an actor, too, perhaps—if I see a chance.

QUINCE
Speak, Pyramus. Thisby, come forward.

BOTTOM
65 Thisby, the flowers have odious sweet aromas—

QUINCE
Odorous! Odorous!

BOTTOM
Odor's sweet aromas.
So does your breath, my dearest Thisby dear.
But listen, a voice! You stay here awhile.
70 And soon I will be back.
He exits.

PUCK
Never before has a stranger Pyramus than this been played!
He exits.

FLUTE
Should I speak now?

QUINCE
Yes, indeed you should. For you see he's just going to investigate a noise that he heard. He will be back.

FLUTE

75 "Most radiant Pyramus, most lily-white of hue,
Of colour like the red rose on triumphant brier,
Most brisky juvenal and eke most lovely Jew,
As true as truest horse that yet would never tire,
I'll meet thee, Pyramus, at Ninny's tomb."

QUINCE

80 "Ninus' tomb," man. Why, you must not speak that yet; that you answer to Pyramus. You speak all your part at once, cues and all. Pyramus enter. Your cue is past; it is, "never tire."

FLUTE

O,—"As true as truest horse, that yet would never tire."

Re-enter ROBIN GOODFELLOW, *and* BOTTOM *with an ass's head.*

BOTTOM

"If I were fair, Thisby, I were only thine."

QUINCE

85 O monstrous! O strange! we are haunted.
Pray, masters, fly, masters! Help!

Exeunt QUINCE, SNUG, FLUTE, SNOUT, *and* STARVELING.

ROBIN GOODFELLOW

I'll follow you, I'll lead you about, around,
Through bog, through bush, through brake, through brier.
Sometime a horse I'll be, sometime a hound,
90 A hog, a headless bear, sometime a fire;
And neigh, and bark, and grunt, and roar, and burn,
Like horse, hound, hog, bear, fire, at every turn.
[*Exit.*]

BOTTOM

Why do they run away? This is a knavery of them to make me afeard.

Re-enter SNOUT.

---

77 *Jew* probably Thisby's meaningless addition to repeat the sound of "juvenal."
80 *Ninus* the ruler of Babylon (and locale of the troop's play).

FLUTE

75 Most radiant Pyramus, so lily-white,
You are the color of a red rose on a triumphant brier.
You are a most lively youth, and also a most lovely Jew.
You are as true as the truest horse, that never tires.
I'll meet you, Pyramus, at Ninny's tomb.

QUINCE

80 "Ninus' tomb," man! Why, you mustn't say that yet. That
is your response to Pyramus. You speak all of your part
at once, cues
and all. Pyramus, enter. Your cue has past. It is "never tire."

FLUTE

O—as true as truest horse that never tires.

Re-enter PUCK *and* BOTTOM *with an ass's head on.*

BOTTOM

If I were handsome, Thisby, I would be yours alone.

QUINCE *sees* BOTTOM *with the ass's head.*

QUINCE

85 O this is monstrous! strange! We are haunted.
Please, gentlemen! Run, gentlemen! Help!

They all exit, except BOTTOM.

PUCK

I'll follow you. I'll lead you roundabout
Through swamp, through bushes, through thickets, through
briers.
Sometimes I'll be a horse, sometimes a hound,
90 A hog, a headless bear, sometimes a fire.
I'll neigh, and bark, and grunt, and roar, and burn,
Like a horse, hound, hog, bear, and fire at every turn.

He exits.

BOTTOM

Why are they running away? This is mean of them to
scare me.

SNOUT *enters.*

SNOUT

95 O Bottom, thou art chang'd! What do I see on thee?

BOTTOM

What do you see? You see an ass-head of your own, do you?

[*Exit* SNOUT.]

Re-enter QUINCE.

QUINCE

Bless thee, Bottom! bless thee! thou art translated.

[*Exit.*]

BOTTOM

I see their knavery; this is to make an ass of me, to fright me, if they could. But I will not stir from this place, do what they
100 can. I will walk up and down here, and I will sing, that they shall hear I am not afraid.

[*Sings.*]

"The ousel cock so black of hue,
With orange-tawny bill,
The throstle with his note so true,
105 The wren with little quill,"—

TITANIA

[*Awaking.*] What angel wakes me from my flowery bed?

BOTTOM

[*Sings.*]

"The finch, the sparrow, and the lark,
The plain-song cuckoo gray,
Whose note full many a man doth mark,
110 And dares not answer nay;"—

for indeed, who would set his wit to so foolish a bird? Who would give a bird the lie, though he cry "cuckoo" never so?

TITANIA

I pray thee, gentle mortal, sing again.
Mine ear is much enamour'd of thy note;
115 So is mine eye enthralled to thy shape;
And thy fair virtue's force perforce doth move me
On the first view to say, to swear, I love thee.

---

105 *quill* a musical reed pipe. 108 *cuckoo* the song of the cuckoo supposedly told a man if he was a cuckold. A cuckold is a man whose wife is an adulteress. (The word "cuckoo" also sounds like cuckold.)

SNOUT
95 O, Bottom, you have changed! What do I see on you?

BOTTOM
What do you see? You're making an ass out of yourself
trying to make one of me, aren't you?
SNOUT *exits.*
QUINCE *enters.*

QUINCE
Heavens, Bottom! Heavens! You've been transformed.
QUINCE *exits.*

BOTTOM
I see what mischief they're up to. They're doing this to make an
ass of me, to frighten me,
if they could. But I won't budge from this place, no matter
what they
100 do. I will walk up and down here, and I will sing so that they shall
hear that I am not afraid:
(He sings.)
The blackbird is very black
And has an orange-tawny bill.
The thrush has a note so true.
105 The wren has a high voice—

TITANIA *(Awakening)*
What angel awakes me from my flowery bed?

BOTTOM *(Singing)*
The finch, the sparrow, and the lark,
The simple-singing gray cuckoo,
To whose note many a man listens
110 And dares not deny—
For, indeed, who would try to reason out an answer to such
a foolish bird? Who would
contradict a bird, even if he does cry "cuckoo" as never before?

TITANIA
I beg you, gentle mortal, sing again.
My ear is very much attracted to your song.
115 My eye also is enslaved by your looks.
And the power of your wonderful character moves me
to say, to swear, that after just one look—I love you.

BOTTOM

Methinks, mistress, you should have little reason for that; and yet, to say the truth; reason and love keep little company together
120 nowadays; the more the pity that some honest neighbours will not make them friends. Nay, I can gleek upon occasion.

TITANIA

Thou art as wise as thou art beautiful.

BOTTOM

Not so, neither; but if I had wit enough to get out of this wood, I have enough to serve mine own turn.

TITANIA

125 Out of this wood do not desire to go;
Thou shalt remain here, whether thou wilt or no.
I am a spirit of no common rate;
The summer still doth tend upon my state;
And I do love thee; therefore, go with me.
130 I'll give thee fairies to attend on thee,
And they shall fetch thee jewels from the deep,
And sing while thou on pressed flowers dost sleep.
And I will purge thy mortal grossness so
That thou shalt like an airy spirit go.
135 Peaseblossom! Cobweb! Moth! and Mustardseed!

Enter four Fairies, PEASEBLOSSOM, COBWEB, MOTH, *and* MUSTARDSEED.

PEASEBLOSSOM

Ready.

COBWEB

And I.

MOTH

And I.

MUSTARDSEED

And I.

ALL

140 Where shall we go?

---

135 *Moth* probably named after "mote" (a small speck of dust) rather than the bug the moth.

BOTTOM

I think, my lady, that you have little reason for that. And
yet, to tell the truth, reason and love aren't often found together
120 these days. It's a pity that some honest neighbors will
not make them friends. You see, I can make a satirical joke upon occasion.

TITANIA

You are as wise as you are beautiful.

BOTTOM

That isn't true either. But if I had enough intelligence to get out of this woods,
I'd have enough to suit myself.

TITANIA

125 Don't desire to leave this woods.
You shall remain here whether you want to or not.
I am no spirit of common rank—
the summer always waits upon me.
And I do love you. Therefore, come with me.
130 I'll give you fairies to wait upon you.
They shall bring you jewels from the deep sea
and sing while you sleep on pressed flowers.
And I will so purify your human grossness,
that you will be able to move like an airy spirit.
135 Peaseblossom! Cobweb! Moth! Mustardseed!

Enter four fairies: PEASEBLOSSOM, COBWEB, MOTH, *and* MUSTARDSEED.

PEASEBLOSSOM

At your service.

COBWEB

And I.

MOTH

And I.

MUSTARDSEED

And I.

ALL

140 Where do you want us to go?

TITANIA
Be kind and courteous to this gentleman.
Hop in his walks and gambol in his eyes;
Feed him with apricocks and dewberries,
With purple grapes, green figs, and mulberries;
145 The honey-bags steal from the humble-bees,
And for night-tapers crop their waxen thighs
And light them at the fiery glow-worm's eyes,
To have my love to bed and to arise;
And pluck the wings from painted butterflies
150 To fan the moonbeams from his sleeping eyes.
Nod to him, elves, and do him courtesies.

PEASEBLOSSOM
Hail, mortal!

COBWEB
Hail!

MOTH
Hail!

MUSTARDSEED
155 Hail!

BOTTOM
I cry your worships mercy, heartily. I beseech your worship's name.

COBWEB
Cobweb.

BOTTOM
I shall desire you of more acquaintance, good Master Cobweb. If I cut my finger, I shall make bold with you. Your name, honest
160 gentleman?

PEASEBLOSSOM
Peaseblossom.

BOTTOM
I pray you commend me to Mistress Squash, your mother, and to Master Peascod, your father. Good Master Peaseblossom, I shall desire you of more acquaintance too. Your name, I beseech
165 you, sir?

---

159 *I shall make bold with you* Cobwebs were used to stop bleeding. 162 *Squash* an unripe peapod. 163 *Peascod* a ripe peapod.

TITANIA
Be kind and courteous to this gentleman.
Hop in his walks and frolic in his eyes.
Feed him with apricots, blackberries,
purple grapes, green figs, and mulberries.
45 Steal the honey bags from the bumblebees,
and for night candles, cut off their waxen thighs
and light them from the fiery glowworm's eyes
to light my love the way to bed and to arise.
Pluck the wings from painted butterflies
50 to fan the moonbeams from his sleeping eyes.
Bow to him, elves, and serve him courteously.

PEASEBLOSSOM
Greetings, mortal!

COBWEB
Greetings!

MOTH
Greetings!

MUSTARDSEED
55 Greetings!

BOTTOM
I heartily beg your pardon, your honors. Please tell me your name, your worship.

COBWEB
Cobweb.

BOTTOM
I want to get to know you better, good Master Cobweb.
If I cut my finger, I will have to ask for your help. What is your name, honest
60 gentleman?

PEASEBLOSSOM
Peaseblossom.

BOTTOM
I beg you, give my regards to Mistress Squash, your mother, and
to Master Peascod, your father. Good Master Peaseblossom, I
want to get to know you better, too. What is your name please,
65 sir?

MUSTARDSEED
Mustardseed.

BOTTOM
Good Master Mustardseed, I know your patience well. That same cowardly, giant-like ox-beef hath devoured many a gentleman of your house. I promise you your kindred hath made my eyes water
170 ere now. I desire you more acquaintance, good Master Mustardseed.

TITANIA
Come, wait upon him; lead him to my bower.
The moon methinks looks with a wat'ry eye;
And when she weeps, weeps every little flower,
175 Lamenting some enforced chastity.
Tie up my love's tongue, bring him silently.
[*Exeunt.*]

Act III, Scene ii: [*Another part of the wood.*] *Enter* OBERON.

OBERON
I wonder if Titania be awak'd;
Then, what it was that next came in her eye,
Which she must dote on in extremity.
Enter ROBIN GOODFELLOW.
Here comes my messenger.
5 How now, mad spirit!
What night-rule now about this haunted grove?

ROBIN GOODFELLOW
My mistress with a monster is in love.
Near to her close and consecrated bower,
While she was in her dull and sleeping hour,
10 A crew of patches, rude mechanicals,
That work for bread upon Athenian stalls,
Were met together to rehearse a play
Intended for great Theseus' nuptial-day.
The shallowest thickskin of that barren sort,
15 Who Pyramus presented in their sport,
Forsook his scene and ent'red in a brake.

168-69 *ox-beef . . . house* mustard was frequently eaten with beef.

MUSTARDSEED
Mustardseed.

BOTTOM
Good Master Mustardseed, I'm well aware of your patient suffering. The
cowardly, giantlike ox-beef has devoured many gentlemen from
your house. I swear to you, your relatives have made my eyes water
170 before now. I want to get to know you better, good Master
Mustardseed.

TITANIA
Come, take care of him. Lead him to my bedroom.
I think the moon is gazing (on the world) with a watery eye.
And when she cries, every little flower cries,
175 Mourning that someone's virginity has been violated.
Tie up my lover's tongue and bring him silently.
All exit.

Act III, Scene ii: Another part of the forest. Enter OBERON.

OBERON
I wonder if Titania has awakened.
If so, I wonder what she first saw,
which she must love to the extreme?
Enter PUCK.
Here comes my messenger.
5 What's going on, mad spirit?
What is happening tonight in this haunted woods?

PUCK
My mistress is in love with a monster.
Near her private and consecrated bower,
while she was resting and sleeping,
10 there came a group of fools—uneducated artisans
who work for bread in Athens.
They had come together to rehearse a play
to be presented on the great Theseus' wedding day.
The shallowest country clown in that stupid crew—
15 who played Pyramus in their little play—
left the "stage" and entered into the thicket.

When I did him at this advantage take,
An ass's nole I fixed on his head.
Anon his Thisby must be answered,
20 And forth my mimic comes. When they him spy,
As wild geese that the creeping fowler eye,
Or russet-pated choughs, many in sort,
Rising and cawing at the gun's report,
Sever themselves and madly sweep the sky,
25 So, at his sight, away his fellows fly;
And, at our stamp, here o'er and o'er one falls;
He murder cries, and help from Athens calls.
Their sense thus weak, lost with their fears thus strong,
Made senseless things begin to do them wrong;
30 For briers and thorns at their apparel snatch;
Some sleeves, some hats, from yielders all things catch.
I led them on in this distracted fear,
And left sweet Pyramus translated there;
When in that moment, so it came to pass,
35 Titania wak'd and straightway lov'd an ass.

OBERON
This falls out better than I could devise.
But hast thou yet latch'd the Athenian's eyes
With the love-juice, as I did bid thee do?

ROBIN GOODFELLOW
I took him sleeping,—that is finish'd too,—
40 And the Athenian woman by his side;
That, when he wak'd, of force she must be ey'd.

Enter DEMETRIUS *and* HERMIA.

OBERON
Stand close; this is the same Athenian.

ROBIN GOODFELLOW
This is the woman, but not this man.

DEMETRIUS
O, why rebuke you him that loves you so?
45 Lay breath so bitter on your bitter foe.

When I was able to catch him at this opportunity,
I secured an ass's head on his shoulders.
Soon he had to answer his Thisby (in the play)
20 and so out comes my clown. When they saw him,
(they ran) like wild geese who see the eye of a concealed hunter.
Or like a large flock of gray-headed jackdaws—
taking off and cawing when the gun goes off,
separating themselves and madly sweeping the sky—
just in that manner his friends flew away at the sight of him.
25 And because of my creature, one of them tumbled over.
Another cried, "Murder," and called for help from Athens.
With their weak brains, and consumed by intense fear,
they imagined that objects could harm them
30 because briers and thorns snatched at their clothes.
Some were caught by their sleeves and hats—cowards are
attacked by everything.
I led them on in this state of wild fear
and left sweet Pyramus changed there.
In that moment, it so happened
35 that Titania awakened and right away fell in love with an ass.

OBERON
This worked out better than I could have planned it.
But have you smeared the Athenian's eyes
with the love juice, as I ordered you to do?

PUCK
I caught him sleeping, so that is finished, too.
40 And the Athenian woman was by his side
so that when he wakes up, by necessity, she will be seen.
Enter DEMETRIUS *and* HERMIA.

OBERON
Hide. This is that very Athenian.

PUCK
This is the woman (I was talking about), but this is not the man.

DEMETRIUS
O why do you scold the man who loves you so much?
45 Save your bitter words for your bitter enemy.

HERMIA

Now I but chide; but I should use thee worse,
For thou, I fear, hast given me cause to curse.
If thou hast slain Lysander in his sleep,
Being o'er shoes in blood, plunge in knee-deep,
50 And kill me too.
The sun was not so true unto the day
As he to me: would he have stolen away
From sleeping Hermia? I'll believe as soon
This whole earth may be bor'd and that the moon
55 May through the centre creep and so displease
Her brother's noontide with the Antipodes.
It cannot be but thou hast murd'red him;
So should a murderer look, so dread, so grim.

DEMETRIUS

So should the murd'red look, and so should I,
60 Pierc'd through the heart with your stern cruelty;
Yet you, the murderer, look as bright, as clear,
As yonder Venus in her glimmering sphere.

HERMIA

What's this to my Lysander? Where is he?
Ah, good Demetrius, wilt thou give him me?

DEMETRIUS

65 I had rather give his carcass to my hounds.

HERMIA

Out, dog! out, cur! thou driv'st me past the bounds
Of maiden's patience. Hast thou slain him, then?
Henceforth be never numb'red among men!
O, once tell true, tell true, even for my sake!
70 Durst thou have look'd upon him being awake,
And has thou kill'd him sleeping? O brave touch!
Could not a worm, an adder, do so much?
An adder did it; for with doubler tongue
Than thine, thou serpent, never adder stung.

---

56 *brother* the sun god was the brother of the moon goddess in Greek mythology.
56 *Antipodes* the people who lived on the other side of the world.

HERMIA

I am only scolding now, but I should treat you worse,
for you, I'm afraid, have given me reason to curse.
If you killed Lysander in his sleep,
and walked ankle-deep in his blood, go ahead
50 and kill me too.
The sun was not as true to the day
as he is to me. Would he have sneaked away
from his sleeping Hermia? I'd as soon believe
that the solid world could be drilled straight through and
that the moon
55 could creep through the center and disrupt
her brother's noontime for the Antipodes.
It has to be that you have murdered him.
You look like a murderer—so deathly pale, so grim.

DEMETRIUS

That is the way the murdered should look, and so should I.
60 I am pierced through the heart by your stern cruelty.
Yet you, the murderer, look as bright and clear
as Venus over there in her glimmering orbit.

HERMIA

What does this have to do with my Lysander? Where is he?
Good Demetrius, won't you give him to me?

DEMETRIUS

65 I'd rather give his dead body to my hounds.

HERMIA

Get away, you dog! Away, you cur! You're driving me beyond the
bounds
of my maidenly patience. Have you killed him, then?
From now on, you should never be called a man.
Tell me the truth just for once! Tell me the truth, for my sake.
70 Would you have even dared look at him if he was awake?
And did you kill him while he slept? What a noble exploit!
Couldn't a snake or an adder do the same?
An adder did do it, for with never a more double tongue
than yours, you snake, did an adder ever sting.

DEMETRIUS
75 You spend your passion on a mispris'd mood.
I am not guilty of Lysander's blood;
Nor is he dead, for aught that I can tell.

HERMIA
I pray thee, tell me then that he is well.

DEMETRIUS
An if I could, what should I get therefore?

HERMIA
80 A privilege never to see me more.
And from thy hated presence part I so:
See me no more, whether he be dead or no.
[*Exit.*]

DEMETRIUS
There is no following her in this fierce vein;
Here therefore for a while I will remain.
85 So sorrow's heaviness doth heavier grow
For debt that bankrupt sleep doth sorrow owe;
Which now in some slight measure it will pay,
If for his tender here I make some stay.
[*Lies down and sleeps.*]

OBERON
What hast thou done? Thou hast mistaken quite
90 And laid the love-juice on some true-love's sight.
Of thy misprision must perforce ensue
Some true love turn'd and not a false turn'd true.

ROBIN GOODFELLOW
Then fate o'er-rules, that, one man holding troth,
A million fail, confounding oath on oath.

OBERON
95 About the wood go swifter than the wind,
And Helena of Athens look thou find.
All fancy-sick she is and pale of cheer
With sighs of love, that costs the fresh blood dear.
By some illusion see thou bring her here.
100 I'll charm his eyes against she do appear.

---

98 *with sighs . . . dear* it was believed that sighs drained blood from the heart.

DEMETRIUS

75 You're wasting your energy in mistaken anger.
I am not guilty of killing Lysander.
Nor is he dead, for all I know.

HERMIA

I beg you, then, tell me he is all right.

DEMETRIUS

If I could, what would I get in return?

HERMIA

80 The privilege of never seeing me again.
And from your hated presence, I will depart.
Don't try to see me again, whether he is dead or not.
She exits.

DEMETRIUS

There is no use following her when she is so angry.
Therefore, I'll stay here for a while.
85 My sorrow grows heavier,
because my sorrow has kept me from sleeping lately.
I will now pay back that debt to a slight extent
if I lie down here and offer myself up to sleep.
(He lies down and goes to sleep.)

OBERON

What have you done? You have made a terrible mistake
90 and laid the love juice on a true lover's eyes.
Your mistakes have resulted in
the estrangement of one true lover and the creation of a true lover.

PUCK

Then fate will overrule us. For each man who remains true,
a million will fail and break vow after vow.

OBERON

95 Go through these woods, swifter than the wind,
and see that you find Helena of Athens.
She is lovesick and her face is pale
from sighing, which dangerously saps her blood.
By some magic, see that you bring her here.
100 I'll charm his eyes in anticipation of her reappearance.

ROBIN GOODFELLOW
I go, I go; look how I go,
Swifter than arrow from the Tartar's bow.
[*Exit.*]

OBERON
Flower of this purple dye,
Hit with Cupid's archery,
105 Sink in apple of his eye.
When his love he doth espy,
Let her shine as gloriously
As the Venus of the sky.
When thou wak'st, if she be by,
110 Beg of her for remedy.
Re-enter ROBIN GOODFELLOW.

ROBIN GOODFELLOW
Captain of our fairy band,
Helena is here at hand;
And the youth, mistook by me,
Pleading for a lover's fee.
115 Shall we their fond pageant see?
Lord, what fools these mortals be!

OBERON
Stand aside. The noise they make
Will cause Demetrius to awake.

ROBIN GOODFELLOW
Then will two at once woo one;
120 That must needs be sport alone.
And those things do best please me
That befall preposterously.
Enter LYSANDER *and* HELENA.

LYSANDER
Why should you think that I should woo in scorn?
Scorn and derision never come in tears.
125 Look when I vow, I weep; and vows so born,
In their nativity all truth appears.
How can these things in me seem scorn to you,
Bearing the badge of faith, to prove them true?

---

102 *Tartar* a warrior of a Turkish or Mongolian tribe from Asia.

PUCK
I'm going, I'm going! See, I'm off like a shot!
Swifter than an arrow from the Tartar's bow.
Exit.

OBERON
Flower of this purple dye,
Hit him as if aimed by Cupid,
105 Sink into the apple of his eye.
When he sees his love,
Let her shine as gloriously
As Venus in the sky.
When you awake, if she is near,
110 Beg her for the cure.
(He puts the juice into Demetrius' eyes.)
Re-enter PUCK.

PUCK
Captain of our fairy band,
Helena is nearby.
And the youth I, mistakenly, daubed with love juice
Is begging her to love him.
115 Shall we watch their silly exhibition?
Lord, what fools these mortals are!

OBERON
Stand aside. The noise they make
Will cause Demetrius to wake.

PUCK
Then the two of them will pursue one girl.
120 That will be supreme fun.
Those things most please me.
That are most preposterous.
Enter LYSANDER *and* HELENA.

LYSANDER
Why do you think I'm courting you in scorn?
Scorn and derision are never accompanied by tears.
125 Look, when I swear to you, I weep. Promises born like that,
Show themselves completely true from in their birth.
How can these things seem like scorn to you
When this sign of loyalty (my tears) proves them to be true?

HELENA
You do advance your cunning more and more.
130 When truth kills truth, O devilish-holy fray!
These vows are Hermia's; will you give her o'er?
Weigh oath with oath, and you will nothing weigh.
Your vows to her and me, put in two scales,
Will even weigh, and both as light as tales.

LYSANDER
135 I had no judgement when to her I swore.

HELENA
Nor none, in my mind, now you give her o'er.

LYSANDER
Demetrius loves her, and he loves not you.

DEMETRIUS
[*Awaking.*] O Helen, goddess, nymph, perfect, divine!
To what, my love, shall I compare thine eyne?
140 Crystal is muddy. O, how ripe in show
Thy lips, those kissing cherries, tempting grow!
That pure congealed white, high Taurus' snow,
Fann'd with the eastern wind, turns to a crow
When thou hold'st up thy hand. O, let me kiss
145 This princess of pure white, this seal of bliss!

HELENA
O spite! O hell! I see you all are bent
To set against me for your merriment.
If you were civil and knew courtesy,
You would not do me thus much injury.
150 Can you not hate me, as I know you do,
But you must join in souls to mock me too?
If you were men, as men you are in show,
You would not use a gentle lady so;
To vow, and swear, and superpraise my parts,
155 When I am sure you hate me with your hearts.
You both are rivals, and love Hermia;
And now both rivals, to mock Helena.
A trim exploit, a manly enterprise,

---

142 *Taurus* a mountain range in Turkey.

HELENA
You display your cleverness more and more.
130 When truth kills truth, what a terrible battle erupts between true and false!
You're giving me the promises you gave to Hermia. Will you desert her?
If you weigh the one promise with the other, you will have nothing to weigh.
Your vows to her, if you put them in two scales,
Would weigh the same—both are as light as lies.

LYSANDER
135 I had no judgment when I swore to her.

HELENA
And you don't have any, in my opinion, now that you're throwing her over.

LYSANDER
Demetrius loves her, and he doesn't love you.

DEMETRIUS *(Awakening)*
O Helen, goddess, nymph, perfect, divine!
To what, my love, shall I compare your eyes?
140 Crystal is muddy in comparison. O, how ripe in appearance
are your lips, like kissing cherries, growing so temptingly!
The pure congealed white of the high Taurus Mountains' snow,
fanned with the eastern winds, turns as black as a crow
when compared to your hand. O let me kiss
145 this princess of pure white, this pledge of bliss!
(He reaches for her hand.)

HELENA
O spiteful men! O hell! I see you all are determined
to turn against me for your own pleasure.
If you were civilized and had any manners,
you would not hurt me like this.
150 Can't you just hate me, as I know you do,
without having to scheme together to mock me too?
If you were men, as men you appear to be,
you would not mistreat a well-bred lady like this.
You promise and swear and overpraise my qualities
155 when I am sure you hate me with all your hearts.
You are both rivals, and you love Hermia.
Now you're both rivals in mocking me.
It is a wonderful deed, a manly enterprise,

To conjure tears up in a poor maid's eyes
160 With your derision! None of noble sort
Would so offend a virgin and extort
A poor soul's patience, all to make you sport.

LYSANDER
You are unkind, Demetrius; be not so;
For you love Hermia; this you know I know.
165 And here, with all good will, with all my heart,
In Hermia's love I yield you up my part;
And yours of Helena to me bequeath,
Whom I do love and will do till my death.

HELENA
Never did mockers waste more idle breath.

DEMETRIUS
170 Lysander, keep thy Hermia; I will none.
If e'er I lov'd her, all that love is gone.
My heart to her but as guest-wise sojourn'd,
And now to Helen is it home return'd,
There to remain.

LYSANDER
175 Helen, it is not so.

DEMETRIUS
Disparage not the faith thou dost not know,
Lest, to thy peril, thou aby it dear.
Look, where thy love comes, yonder is thy dear.

Re-enter HERMIA.

HERMIA
Dark night, that from the eye his function takes,
180 The ear more quick of apprehension makes;
Wherein it doth impair the seeing sense,
It pays the hearing double recompense.
Thou art not by mine eye, Lysander, found;
Mine ear, I thank it, brought me to thy sound.
185 But why unkindly didst thou leave me so?

to bring tears to a poor maiden's eyes
160 with your scorn. No one who was of real nobility
would offend a maiden like this and torture
a poor soul's patience, just to entertain you.

LYSANDER
You are unkind, Demetrius. Don't be unkind!
You love Hermia; you know I know that.
165 And here, with all good will, with all my heart,
I give up my part of Hermia's love to you.
You give me your love for Helena,
whom I love and will love her until I die.

HELENA
I have never seen mockers waste such useless breath.

DEMETRIUS
170 Lysander, keep your Hermia—I don't want any part of her.
If I ever loved her, all that love is gone.
My heart merely visited her as a guest,
and now it has returned home to Helena
where it will remain.

LYSANDER
175 Helena, this is not true.

DEMETRIUS
Don't put down a faith you don't know,
or you may pay dearly for it to your regret.
Look, your love is coming. There is your dear one.
Enter HERMIA.

HERMIA
Dark night, that makes the eyes useless,
180 makes the ear quicker to understand.
While it weakens the sense of sight,
it makes up for that by doubling the ability to hear.
I did not find you with my eyes, Lysander.
It's thanks to my ears for bringing me to your sound.
185 But why did you so unkindly leave me like that?

LYSANDER
Why should he stay, whom love doth press to go?

HERMIA
What love could press Lysander from my side?

LYSANDER
Lysander's love, that would not let him bide,
Fair Helena, who more engilds the night
190 Than all yon fiery oes and eyes of light.
Why seek'st thou me? Could not this make thee know,
The hate I bare thee made me leave thee so?

HERMIA
You speak not as you think. It cannot be.

HELENA
Lo, she is one of this confederacy!
195 Now I perceive they have conjoin'd all three
To fashion this false sport, in spite of me.
Injurious Hermia! most ungrateful maid!
Have you conspir'd, have you with these contriv'd
To bait me with this foul derision?
200 Is all the counsel that we two have shar'd,
The sisters' vows, the hours that we have spent,
When we have chid the hasty-footed time
For parting us,—O, is all forgot?
All school-days' friendship, childhood innocence?
205 We, Hermia, like two artificial gods,
Have with our needles created both one flower,
Both on one sampler, sitting on one cushion,
Both warbling of one song, both in one key,
As if our hands, our sides, voices and minds
210 Had been incorporate. So we grew together,
Like to a double cherry, seeming parted,
But yet an union in partition;
Two lovely berries moulded on one stem;
So, with two seeming bodies but one heart;
215 Two of the first, like coats in heraldry,
Due but to one and crowned with one crest.

---

190 *fiery . . . light* Lysander is referring to the stars. 215 *Two of the first* is a term to describe a shield where two coats of arms appeared, such as that of man and wife, under one crest.

LYSANDER
Why should anyone stay when love urges them to go?

HERMIA
What love could urge Lysander to leave me?

LYSANDER
My love, that would not let me stay—
lovely Helena, who decorates the night more
190 than all those fiery circles and eyes of light.
Why did you seek me out? Doesn't this tell you that the
hate I bear towards you made me leave you like that?

HERMIA
You are not saying what you mean. It cannot be.

HELENA
So, she is a part of this plot!
195 Now I see that all three of them have joined together
to carry out this false game to spite me.
Insulting Hermia! You most ungrateful maiden!
Have you conspired, have you plotted with these two
to torture me with this disgusting scorn?
200 Are all the private conversations that we two shared,
the sisters' vows, the hours we have spent
scolding hasty-footed time
for parting us—is all of that forgotten?
Have you forgotten our schoolday's friendship and
childhood innocence?
205 We, Hermia, like two artistic gods,
have together created one flower with our separate needles
on one piece of embroidery, sitting on one cushion,
both singing one song in the same key.
It was as if our hands, our sides, our voices, and our minds,
210 had been joined in one body. We grew together,
like a double cherry, seemingly separate,
yet united even though we were in two parts—
two lovely berries growing from one stem.
In the same way, we seem to have two bodies but one heart.
215 We are like a shield with two coats of arms
crowned by a single crest.

And will you rend our ancient love asunder,
To join with men in scorning your poor friend?
It is not friendly, 'tis not maidenly.
220 Our sex, as well as I, may chide you for it,
Though I alone do feel the injury.

HERMIA
I am amazed at your passionate words.
I scorn you not; it seems that you scorn me.

HELENA
Have you not set Lysander, as in scorn,
225 To follow me and praise my eyes and face?
And made your other love, Demetrius,
Who even but now did spurn me with his foot,
To call me goddess, nymph, divine and rare,
Precious, celestial? Wherefore speaks he this
230 To her he hates? And wherefore doth Lysander
Deny your love, so rich within his soul,
And tender me, forsooth, affection,
But by your setting on, by your consent?
What though I be not so in grace as you,
235 So hung upon with love, so fortunate,
But miserable most, to love unlov'd?
This you should pity rather than despise.

HERMIA
I understand not what you mean by this.

HELENA
Ay, do, persever, counterfeit sad looks,
240 Make mouths upon me when I turn my back,
Wink each at other, hold the sweet jest up;
This sport, well carried, shall be chronicled.
If you have any pity, grace, or manners,
You would not make me such an argument.
245 But fare ye well; 'tis partly my own fault,
Which death or absence soon shall remedy.

Will you tear our old love apart
to join with these men in scorning your poor friend?
That is not friendly; that is not maidenly!
20 Apart from me, every other woman could scold you for it,
though I alone have been hurt.

HERMIA

Your passionate words have left me speechless.
I'm not scorning you. I think you're scorning me.

HELENA

Haven't you egged on Lysander to scorn me
25 by following me and praising my eyes and face?
And didn't you make your other love, Demetrius,
(who just awhile ago spurned me with his foot)
call me goddess, nymph, divine, unique,
precious, and celestial? Why would he say this
30 to someone he hates? And why does Lysander
deny his love for you—that love which fills his soul—
and offer me his affection,
unless you urged him on and agreed to it?
What does it matter if I am not as popular as you are,
35 or as loved or as fortunate,
instead of being the most miserable and unloved person alive?
You should pity me for that reason rather than despise me.

HERMIA

I don't understand what you mean by this.

HELENA

Oh, go ahead! Go on, fake those grave looks,
40 make faces at me when I turn my back,
wink at each other, keep up the delightful joking.
This joke, if you carry it off well, will be legendary.
If you have any pity, goodness, or manners,
you would not make me the subject of such scorn.
45 But goodbye. This is partly my own fault—
which either my death or my absence will soon remedy.

LYSANDER
Stay, gentle Helena; hear my excuse,
My love, my life, my soul, fair Helena!

HELENA
O excellent!

HERMIA
250 Sweet, do not scorn her so.

DEMETRIUS
If she cannot entreat, I can compel.

LYSANDER
Thou canst compel no more than she entreat.
Thy threats have no more strength than her weak prayers.
Helen, I love thee; by my life, I do!
255 I swear by that which I will lose for thee,
To prove him false that says I love thee not.

DEMETRIUS
I say I love thee more than he can do.

LYSANDER
If thou say so, withdraw, and prove it too.

DEMETRIUS
Quick, come!

HERMIA
260 Lysander, whereto tends all this?

LYSANDER
Away, you Ethiope!

DEMETRIUS
No, no; he'll but
Seem to break loose. Take on as you would follow,
But yet come not. You are a tame man, go!

LYSANDER
265 Hang off, thou cat, thou burr! Vile thing, let loose,
Or I will shake thee from me like a serpent!

---

261 *Ethiope* is a reference to Hermia's brunette hair.

LYSANDER
Stay, noble Helena. Listen to my plea,
my love, my life, my soul, lovely Helena!

HELENA *(Sarcastically)*
O excellent!

HERMIA *(to Lysander)*
250 My sweet, do not scorn her like that.

DEMETRIUS
If she can't persuade you, I can force you (to stop bothering Helena).

LYSANDER
You can't force me any more than she can persuade me.
Your threats have no more effect on me than her weak prayers.
Helena, I love you. I swear by my life, I do!
255 I swear by my life, which I would give up for you
in order to prove anyone a liar who says I don't love you.

DEMETRIUS
And I say that I love you more than he can.

LYSANDER
If you say that, come with me and prove it.

DEMETRIUS
Let's go right now!

HERMIA
260 Lysander, what does all of this mean?
(She grabs him.)

LYSANDER
Get away, you dark woman.
(Tries to shake her off.)

DEMETRIUS *(to Lysander)*
No, no; he'll
pretend to try to break free and act as if he's upset,
but he won't really leave. You are a coward!

LYSANDER *(to Hermia)*
265 Let go, you cat, you burr! You vile thing, let go,
or I will shake you off like I would a snake!

HERMIA
Why are you grown so rude? What change is this?
Sweet love,—

LYSANDER
Thy love! Out, tawny Tartar, out!
270 Out, loathed medicine! O hated potion, hence!

HERMIA
Do you not jest?

HELENA
Yes, sooth; and so do you.

LYSANDER
Demetrius, I will keep my word with thee.

DEMETRIUS
I would I had your bond, for I perceive
275 A weak bond holds you. I'll not trust your word.

LYSANDER
What, should I hurt her, strike her, kill her dead?
Although I hate her, I'll not harm her so.

HERMIA
What, can you do me greater harm than hate?
Hate me! wherefore? O me! what news, my love!
280 Am not I Hermia? Are not you Lysander?
I am as fair now as I was erewhile.
Since night you lov'd me; yet since night you left me:
Why, then you left me—O, the gods forbid!—
In earnest, shall I say?

LYSANDER
285 Ay, by my life;
And never did desire to see thee more.
Therefore be out of hope, of question, doubt;
Be certain, nothing truer; 'tis no jest
That I do hate thee and love Helena.

HERMIA
Why have you grown so rude? What is this change,
my sweet love?

LYSANDER
Your love? Get away, you brown Tartar, away!
270 Away, you hateful medicine! You hated potion, get away!

HERMIA
Surely you're joking?

HELENA
Yes, truly, and so are you.

LYSANDER
Demetrius, I'll keep my promise to fight you.

DEMETRIUS
I wish I had your bond, for I see
275 that even a weak vow holds you. I won't trust your word.

LYSANDER
What do you want me to do? Hurt her, strike her, kill her?
Even though I hate her, I won't harm her like that.

HERMIA
What greater harm can you do me than by hating me?
Hate me? Why? Alas! What is this, my love?
280 Am I not Hermia? Are you not Lysander?
I am as beautiful as I was earlier.
Even up to nightfall you loved me. Yet just since nightfall,
you left me.
So then, you left me—heaven forbid!—
intentionally? Am I right?

LYSANDER
285 Yes, yes!
And I never wanted to see you again.
Therefore, quit hoping, questioning, and doubting.
You can be certain. There's nothing truer. It's no joke
that I hate you and love Helena.

HERMIA

290 O me! you juggler! you canker-blossom!
You thief of love! What, have you come by night
And stolen my love's heart from him?

HELENA

Fine, i' faith!
Have you no modesty, no maiden shame,
295 No touch of bashfulness? What, will you tear
Impatient answers from my gentle tongue?
Fie, fie! you counterfeit, you puppet, you!

HERMIA

"Puppet?" Why so? Ay, that way goes the game.
Now I perceive that she hath made compare
300 Between our statures; she hath urg'd her height;
And with her personage, her tall personage,
Her height, forsooth, she hath prevail'd with him.
And are you grown so high in his esteem,
Because I am so dwarfish and so low?
305 How low am I, thou painted maypole? Speak,
How low am I? I am not yet so low
But that my nails can reach unto thine eyes.

HELENA

I pray you, though you mock me, gentlemen,
Let her not hurt me. I was never curst;
310 I have no gift at all in shrewishness;
I am a right maid for my cowardice.
Let her not strike me. You perhaps may think,
Because she is something lower than myself,
That I can match her.

HERMIA

315 "Lower!" hark, again.

HELENA

Good Hermia, do not be so bitter with me.
I evermore did love you, Hermia,
Did ever keep your counsels, never wrong'd you;
Save that, in love unto Demetrius,

---

290 *canker blossom* probably refers to a worm that destroys the rose blossom.

HERMIA

290 Alas! *(To Helena)* You juggler! You worm!
You thief of love! So, did you come by night
and steal my love's heart away from him?

HELENA

This is fine, indeed!
Don't you have any modesty or shame,
295 no touch of bashfulness? So, will you tear
impatient retorts from my soft-spoken tongue?
For shame! You fake! You puppet, you!

HERMIA

Puppet? Why is that? Oh, so that's the way she wants to play.
Now I see that she's made comparisons
300 between our heights. She has shown off her height,
and with her self, her tall self,
her height, she has won him over.
Have you grown so tall in his esteem
because I am so dwarfish and so short?
305 How short am I, you painted maypole? Answer me!
How short am I? I'm not yet so short
that my nails can't reach your eyes.

HELENA

I beg you, even though you mock me, gentlemen,
don't let her hurt me. I have never been quarrelsome.
310 I don't have a talent for shrewishness.
I am a true young woman in respect to my cowardice.
Don't let her hit me. You perhaps may think
because she is shorter than I am
that I am a match for her.

HERMIA

315 Shorter! She said it again!

HELENA

Good Hermia, don't be so bitter toward me.
I've always loved you, Hermia,
always kept your secrets, never did anything to hurt you—
except, out of love for Demetrius,

320 I told him of your stealth unto this wood.
He followed you; for love I followed him;
But he hath chid me hence and threat'nd me
To strike me, spurn me, nay, to kill me too.
And now, so you will let me quiet go,
325 To Athens will I bear my folly back
And follow you no further. Let me go.
You see how simple and how fond I am.

HERMIA
Why, get you gone; who is't that hinders you?

HELENA
A foolish heart, that I leave here behind.

HERMIA
330 What, with Lysander?

HELENA
With Demetrius.

LYSANDER
Be not afraid; she shall not harm thee, Helena.

DEMETRIUS
No, sir, she shall not, though you take her part.

HELENA
O, when she's angry, she is keen and shrewd!
335 She was a vixen when she went to school;
And though she be but little, she is fierce.

HERMIA
"Little" again! Nothing but "low" and "little"!
Why will you suffer her to flout me thus?
Let me come to her.

LYSANDER
340 Get you gone, you dwarf,
You minimus, of hind'ring knot-grass made;
You bead, you acorn.

---

341 *minimus* the smallest of creatures. 341 *knot-grass* supposedly stunted one's growth.

320 I told him that you had sneaked into this woods.
He followed you. I followed him because I loved him.
But he scolded me to go away and threatened to
strike me, spurn me—yes, even kill me, too.
And now, if you will let me go in peace,
325 I'll take my foolishness back to Athens,
and follow you no more. Let me go.
You see how simple-minded and foolish I am.

HERMIA
Well then, go! Who's stopping you?

HELENA
My foolish heart which I leave behind here.

HERMIA
330 With Lysander?

HELENA
With Demetrius.

LYSANDER
Don't be afraid. She shall not harm you, Helena.

DEMETRIUS
No, sir, she shall not, even though you offer to be her defender.

HELENA
O, when she's angry, she's cruel and shrewish.
335 She was a terror when she went to school.
And though she's small, she's fierce.

HERMIA
"Small" again! Again and again "short" and "small!"
Why do you let her insult me like this?
Let me at her!

LYSANDER
340 Go away, you dwarf!
You must have been fed on knotgrass, you worm!
You bead, you acorn!

DEMETRIUS

You are too officious
In her behalf that scorns your services.
345 Let her alone; speak not of Helena;
Take not her part; for, if thou dost intend
Never so little show of love to her,
Thou shalt aby it.

LYSANDER

Now she holds me not.
350 Now follow, if thou dar'st, to try whose right,
Of thine or mine, is most in Helena.

DEMETRIUS

Follow! Nay, I'll go with thee, cheek by jowl.
[*Exeunt* LYSANDER *and* DEMETRIUS.]

HERMIA

You, mistress, all this coil is 'long of you.
Nay, go not back.

HELENA

355 I will not trust you, I,
Nor longer stay in your curst company.
Your hands than mine are quicker for a fray;
My legs are longer though, to run away.
[*Exit.*]

HERMIA

I am amaz'd, and know not what to say.
[*Exit.*]

OBERON

360 This is thy negligence. Still thou mistak'st,
Or else committ'st thy knaveries wilfully.

ROBIN GOODFELLOW

Believe me, king of shadows, I mistook.
Did not you tell me I should know the man
By the Athenian garments he had on?
365 And so far blameless proves my enterprise,

DEMETRIUS
You are overly concerned
about defending someone who scorns your help.
345 Leave her alone. Don't talk about Helena.
Don't take her side. If you offer
even a little show of love for her,
you'll regret it.

LYSANDER
Hermia isn't holding me back now.
350 So follow me, now, if you dare. We'll see who most deserves
Helena—you or me.

DEMETRIUS
Follow? No, I'll go with you, side by side.
They exit.

HERMIA
You, woman, you are the cause of all this trouble.
—No, don't go back.

HELENA
355 I don't trust you,
nor will I stay any longer in your cruel company.
Your hands are quicker than mine for a fight;
but my legs are longer for running away.
She exits.

HERMIA
I am confused and don't know what to say.
She exits.

OBERON
360 This is all your fault. You're still confusing things
or else making this mischief on purpose.

PUCK
Believe me, king of shadows, it was an accident.
Didn't you tell me I should recognize the man
by the Athenian garments he had on?
365 You see that I am innocent in the way I did my duty

That I have 'nointed an Athenian's eyes;
And so far am I glad it so did sort,
As this their jangling I esteem a sport.

OBERON

Thou see'st these lovers seek a place to fight;
370 Hie therefore, Robin, overcast the night.
The starry welkin cover thou anon
With drooping fog as black as Acheron,
And lead these testy rivals so astray
As one come not within another's way.
375 Like to Lysander sometime frame thy tongue,
Then stir Demetrius up with bitter wrong;
And sometime rail thou like Demetrius;
And from each other look thou lead them thus,
Till o'er their brows death-counterfeiting sleep
380 With leaden legs and batty wings doth creep.
Then crush this herb into Lysander's eye;
Whose liquor hath this virtuous property,
To take from thence all error with his might,
And make his eyeballs roll with wonted sight.
385 When they next wake, all this derision
Shall seem a dream and fruitless vision;
And back to Athens shall the lovers wend
With league whose date till death shall never end.
Whiles I in this affair do thee employ,
390 I'll to my queen and beg her Indian boy;
And then I will her charmed eye release
From monster's view, and all things shall be peace.

ROBIN GOODFELLOW

My fairy lord, this must be done with haste,
For Night's swift dragons cut the clouds full fast,
395 And yonder shines Aurora's harbinger,
At whose approach, ghosts, wand'ring here and there,
Troop home to churchyards. Damned spirits all,
That in crossways and floods have burial,
Already to their wormy beds are gone.

---

372 *Acheron* a river in Hades, the world of the dead in classical mythology. 395 *Auror* the goddess of the dawn. 397-98 *Damned . . . floods* those who had been buried withou holy ceremonies. Suicides were buried at crossroads without church rites becaus

because I did anoint an Athenian's eyes.
And I'm glad it turned out this way
because I think their fighting is entertaining.

OBERON

You heard that these lovers are looking for a place to fight.
370 Therefore, run, Robin, make the night overcast.
Cover the starry sky at once
with drooping fog, as black as the Acheron.
Lead these angry rivals so far apart
that the one will not come near the other.
375 Imitate Lysander's voice sometimes,
and make Demetrius angry with bitter insults.
Then sometimes yell like Demetrius.
Be sure to lead them apart like this
until deathlike sleep comes creeping
380 over their eyes with heavy legs and batlike wings.
Then crush this herb into Lysander's eyes.
Its juice has the valuable quality
of removing all delusions with its power.
It will make his eyes function with their normal sight.
385 When they awake again, all this foolishness
will seem like a dream and an unreal vision.
Then back to Athens the lovers will go,
united in love until death.
While you are taking care of this,
390 I'll go to my queen and ask her for the Indian boy.
And then I will clear her enchanted eyes
of her monstrous delusion, and everything will be peaceful.

PUCK

My fairy lord, this must be done quickly,
for night's swift dragons are swiftly moving through the sky,
395 and over there, the morning star is shining,
at whose approach, ghosts, wandering here and there,
troop home to churchyards. All of the damned spirits
that are buried in the crossroads and water
have already gone to their wormy graves

---

suicide was considered a crime. Drowning victims whose bodies were not recovered were believed to roam the earth because they had not been properly buried.

400 For fear lest day should look their shames upon,
They wilfully themselves exile from light
And must for aye consort with black-brow'd night.

OBERON
But we are spirits of another sort.
I with the Morning's love have oft made sport,
405 And, like a forester, the groves may tread,
Even till the eastern gate, all fiery-red,
Opening on Neptune with fair blessed beams
Turns into yellow gold his salt green streams.
But, notwithstanding, haste, make no delay;
410 We may effect this business yet ere day.
[*Exit.*]

ROBIN GOODFELLOW
Up and down, up and down,
I will lead them up and down.
I am fear'd in field and town.
Goblin, lead them up and down.
415 Here comes one.
Re-enter LYSANDER.

LYSANDER
Where art thou, proud Demetrius? Speak thou now.

ROBIN GOODFELLOW
Here, villain; drawn and ready. Where art thou?

LYSANDER
I will be with thee straight.

ROBIN GOODFELLOW
Follow me, then,
420 To plainer ground.
[*Exit* LYSANDER, *as following the voice.*]
Re-enter DEMETRIUS.

DEMETRIUS
Lysander, speak again!
Thou runaway, thou coward, art thou fled?
Speak! In some bush? Where dost thou hide thy head?

---

404 *Morning's love* either Aurora or her lover, Cephalus.

400 because they do not want the daylight to see their shame.
So, they willfully exile themselves from light
and must forever associate with black-browed night.

OBERON
But we are spirits of another sort.
I have often romped with Morning's love.
405 Like a forester, I walk through the groves
until the (sun in the) eastern sky, all fiery-red,
dawns upon the sea with beautiful blessed beams,
turning the sea's salty green streams to yellow gold.
But hurry now. Do not delay.
410 We may get this business done yet before day.
He exits.

PUCK
Up and down, up and down,
I will lead them up and down.
I am feared in field and town.
I, Hobgoblin, will lead them up and down.
415 Here comes one of them.
Enter LYSANDER.

LYSANDER
Where are you, proud Demetrius? Say something!

PUCK *(Imitating Demetrius)*
Here I am, villain. My sword is drawn and ready. Where are you?

LYSANDER
I'm right behind you.

PUCK *(As Demetrius)*
Follow me, then,
420 to more level ground.
LYSANDER *exits.*
Enter DEMETRIUS.

DEMETRIUS
Lysander, say something again!
You runaway, you coward, have you fled?
Speak! Are you in a bush? Where are you hiding?

ROBIN GOODFELLOW
Thou coward, art thou bragging to the stars,
425 Telling the bushes that thou look'st for wars,
And wilt not come? Come, recreant; come, thou child,
I'll whip thee with a rod. He is defil'd
That draws a sword on thee.

DEMETRIUS
Yea, art thou there?

ROBIN GOODFELLOW
430 Follow my voice. We'll try no manhood here.
[*Exeunt.*]
Re-enter LYSANDER.

LYSANDER
He goes before me and still dares me on.
When I come where he calls, then he is gone.
The villain is much lighter-heel'd than I;
I followed fast, but faster he did fly,
435 That fallen am I in dark uneven way,
And here will rest me. Come, thou gentle day!
[*Lies down.*]
For if but once thou show me thy grey light,
I'll find Demetrius and revenge this spite.
[*Sleeps.*]

Re-enter ROBIN GOODFELLOW *and* DEMETRIUS.

ROBIN GOODFELLOW
Ho, ho, ho! Coward, why com'st thou not?

DEMETRIUS
440 Abide me, if thou dar'st; for well I wot
Thou runn'st before me, shifting every place,
And dar'st not stand, nor look me in the face.
Where art thou now?

ROBIN GOODFELLOW
Come hither; I am here.

427-28 *I'll . . . sword* Puck's taunt implies that it would be unfair to attack a "child" like Demetrius with an adult weapon such as a sword. The only fitting punishment for him would be a spanking.

PUCK *(Imitating Lysander)*
You coward, are you bragging to the stars,
425 telling the bushes that you're looking for a fight,
and yet you won't follow me? Come on, coward! Come on,
you baby.
I'll beat you with a rod. The man is disgraced
who would fight you with a sword.

DEMETRIUS
So, are you there?

PUCK *(As Lysander)*
430 Follow the sound of my voice. We won't test our bravery here.
They exit.
Enter LYSANDER.

LYSANDER
He's ahead of me, always daring me to follow.
When I go where he calls, he's already gone.
The villain is much faster than I am.
I followed him quickly, but he ran even more quickly,
435 so that I have stumbled into this dark, rough place.
And here I will rest. Come, you gentle day!
(He lies down.)
If just once you'll show me your gray light,
I'll find Demetrius and revenge this insult.
(He goes to sleep.)
Enter PUCK *and* DEMETRIUS.

PUCK *(Imitating Lysander)*
Ho, ho, ho! Coward, why aren't you following me?

DEMETRIUS
440 Wait for me, if you dare, for I'm sure
that you are running before me, darting from place to place,
and not daring to stand still or look me in the face.
Where are you now?

PUCK *(As Lysander)*
Come here. I am here.

DEMETRIUS

445 Nay, then, thou mock'st me. Thou shalt buy this dear,
If ever I thy face by daylight see.
Now, go thy way. Faintness constraineth me
To measure out my length on this cold bed.
By day's approach look to be visited.
[*Lies down and sleeps.*]

Re-enter HELENA.

HELENA

450 O weary night, O long and tedious night,
Abate thy hours! Shine, comforts, from the east,
That I may back to Athens by daylight,
From these that my poor company detest.
And sleep, that sometimes shuts up sorrow's eye,
455 Steal me awhile from mine own company.
[*Lies down and sleeps.*]

ROBIN GOODFELLOW

Yet but three? Come one more;
Two of both kinds makes up four.
Re-enter HERMIA.
Here she comes, curst and sad.
Cupid is a knavish lad,
460 Thus to make poor females mad.

HERMIA

Never so weary, never so in woe,
Bedabbled with the dew and torn with briers,
I can no further crawl, no further go;
My legs can keep no pace with my desires.
465 Here will I rest me till the break of day.
Heavens shield Lysander, if they mean a fray!
[*Lies down and sleeps.*]

ROBIN GOODFELLOW

On the ground
Sleep sound.
I'll apply

DEMETRIUS

445 I see; you're mocking me. You'll pay for this dearly
if I ever see your face by daylight.
Now, go away. Exhaustion forces me
to stretch out on this cold ground.
You can be sure I'll find you when daylight comes.
(He lies down and goes to sleep.)
Enter HELENA.

HELENA

450 O weary night, O long and tedious night,
Cut short your hours! Shine some comfort from the east
So I can get back to Athens by daylight,
Away from these people who detest me.
Sleep, that sometimes shuts up sorrow's eyes,
455 Please take me away for a while from my own company.
(She sleeps.)

PUCK

Still only three of them? I need one more.
Two of both sexes make up four.
Enter HERMIA.
Here she comes, cross and sad.
Cupid is a wicked lad
460 To make poor females mad like this.

HERMIA

I have never been so tired or so sad.
I am wet with dew and torn by thorns.
I can't crawl any further or go any further.
My legs can't keep pace with my desires.
465 I will rest here until morning.
May the heavens protect Lysander, if he means to fight.
(She lies down and goes to sleep.)

PUCK

On the ground
Sleep sound.
I'll apply

470 To your eye,
Gentle lover, remedy.
[*Squeezing the juice on Lysander's eyes.*]
When thou wak'st,
Thou tak'st
True delight
475 In the sight
Of thy former lady's eye;
And the country proverb known,
That every man should take his own,
In your waking shall be shown.
480 Jack shall have Jill;
Nought shall go ill;
The man shall have his mare again, and all shall be well.
[*Exit.*]

Act IV, Scene i: [*The same.*] *LYSANDER, DEMETRIUS, HELENA, and HERMIA, lying asleep. Enter* TITANIA *and Clown* BOTTOM; PEASEBLOSSOM, COBWEB, MOTH, MUSTARDSEED, *and other Fairies attending;* OBERON *behind, unseen.*

TITANIA
Come, sit thee down upon this flow'ry bed,
While I thy amiable cheeks do coy;
And stick musk-roses in thy sleek smooth head,
And kiss thy fair large ears, my gentle joy.

BOTTOM
5 Where's Peaseblossom?

PEASEBLOSSOM
Ready.

BOTTOM
Scratch my head, Peaseblossom. Where's Mounsieur Cobweb?

COBWEB
Ready.

470 To your eye,
Gentle lover, a remedy.
(He squeezes the juice on Lysander's eyelids.)
When you wake,
You'll take
True delight
475 In the sight
Of your former lady-love's eyes.
And the well-known country proverb,
that every man must take his own,
will be proven when you awaken.
480 Jack will have his Jill.
Nothing will go ill.
The man will have his mare again, and all will be well.
He exits.

Act IV, Scene i: The woods. LYSANDER, DEMETRIUS, HELENA, *and* HERMIA *are lying asleep. Enter* TITANIA, BOTTOM, *the clown,* PEASEBLOSSOM, COBWEB, MOTH, MUSTARDSEED, *and other fairies, and* OBERON, *behind the rest, unseen.*

TITANIA *(To Bottom)*
Come, sit down upon this flowery bed
While I stroke your lovely cheeks
And stick musk roses in your sleek, smooth head
And kiss your beautiful, large ears, my noble love.

BOTTOM
5 Where's Peaseblossom?

PEASEBLOSSOM
At your service.

BOTTOM
Scratch my head, Peaseblossom. Where's Mr. Cobweb?

COBWEB
At your service.

BOTTOM

Mounsieur Cobweb, good mounsieur, get you your weapons i
10 your hand, and kill me a red-hipp'd humble-bee on the top o
a thistle; and, good mounsieur, bring me the honey-bag. Do no
fret yourself too much in the action, mounsieur, and, good
mounsieur, have a care the honey-bag break not; I would be loat
to have you overflown with a honey-bag, signior. Where'
15 Mounsieur Mustardseed?

MUSTARDSEED

Ready.

BOTTOM

Give me your neaf, Mounsieur Mustardseed. Pray you, leave you
courtesy, good mounsieur.

MUSTARDSEED

What's your will?

BOTTOM

20 Nothing, good mounsieur, but to help Cavalery Cobweb t
scratch. I must to the barber's, mounsieur; for methinks I an
marvellous hairy about the face; and I am such a tender ass, i
my hair do but tickle me, I must scratch.

TITANIA

What, wilt thou hear some music, my sweet love?

BOTTOM

25 I have a reasonable good ear in music. Let's have the tongs an
the bones.

[*Music. Tongs. Rural music.*]

TITANIA

Or say, sweet love, what thou desir'st to eat.

BOTTOM

Truly, a peck of provender; I could munch your good dry oats
Methinks I have a great desire to a bottle of hay. Good hay, swee
30 hay, hath no fellow.

TITANIA

I have a venturous fairy that shall seek
The squirrel's hoard, and fetch for thee new nuts.

25-26 *tongs and the bones* were crude musical instruments of the time.

BOTTOM

Mr. Cobweb, good sir, get your weapons
10 and kill me a red-hipped bumblebee on top of
a thistle. And good sir, bring me the honey bag. Don't
exert yourself too much doing this, sir. And, good
sir, be careful that the honey bag does not break. I would hate
to have you drenched in honey, sir. Where's
15 Mr. Mustardseed?

MUSTARDSEED

At your service.

BOTTOM

Give me your hand, Mr. Mustardseed. Please stop
bowing, good sir.

MUSTARDSEED

What do you wish?

BOTTOM

20 Nothing, good sir, except that you help Cavalier Cobweb to
scratch me. I must go to the barber, sir, for I think I am
amazingly hairy about the face. And I'm such a tender ass that if
my hair tickles me, I have to scratch.

TITANIA

Would you like to hear some music, my sweet love?

BOTTOM

25 I have a reasonably good ear for music. Let's hear the tongs and
the bones.

(Music is played.)

TITANIA

Tell me, my sweet love, what would you like to eat?

BOTTOM

Really, I'd like a peck of dry food. I could munch some
good, dry oats.
I think I really feel like having a bundle of hay. Good hay, sweet
30 hay, has no equal.

TITANIA

I have an adventurous fairy that will find
a squirrel's storehouse and get you some nuts.

BOTTOM

I had rather have a handful or two of dried peas. But, I pray you, let none of your people stir me; I have an exposition of sleep come
35 upon me.

TITANIA

Sleep thou, and I will wind thee in my arms.
Fairies, be gone, and be always away.
[*Exeunt fairies.*]
So doth the woodbine the sweet honeysuckle
Gently entwist; the female ivy so
40 Enrings the barky fingers of the elm.
O, how I love thee! how I dote on thee!
[*They sleep.*]

Enter ROBIN GOODFELLOW.

OBERON

[*Advancing.*] Welcome, good Robin. See'st thou this sweet sight?
Her dotage now I do begin to pity;
For, meeting her of late behind the wood,
45 Seeking sweet favours for this hateful fool,
I did upbraid her and fall out with her.
For she his hairy temples then had rounded
With coronet of fresh and fragrant flowers;
And that same dew, which sometime on the buds
50 Was wont to swell like round and orient pearls,
Stood now within the pretty flowerets' eyes
Like tears that did their own disgrace bewail.
When I had at my pleasure taunted her
And she in mild terms begg'd my patience,
55 I then did ask of her her changeling child;
Which straight she gave me, and her fairy sent
To bear him to my bower in fairy land.
And, now I have the boy, I will undo
This hateful imperfection of her eyes;
60 And, gentle Puck, take this transformed scalp

---

34 *exposition* Bottom's malapropism for "disposition." 39 *female ivy* which depends upon the tree for support like a wife was supposed to depend upon her husband.

BOTTOM

I'd rather have a handful or two of dried peas. But, I beg you,
don't let any of your people bother me. I have an exposition
for sleep
35 now.

TITANIA

Sleep, and I will fold you in my arms.
Fairies, go away. Spread out in every direction.
The fairies exit.
TITANIA *hugs* BOTTOM.
In just this way the woodbine wraps around the honeysuckle
gently. Just like this, the clinging ivy
40 encircles the bark on the branches of the elm.
Oh, how I love you! How I adore you!
(They go to sleep.)
Enter PUCK.

OBERON *(Coming forward)*

Welcome, good Robin. Do you see this sweet sight?
I'm beginning to pity her delusionment.
I met her recently behind the woods
45 as she was searching for sweet love tokens for this hateful fool.
I scolded her and quarreled with her.
She had covered his hairy forehead
with a crown of fresh and fragrant flowers,
and the dew, which once on the flower's buds
50 used to swell like round and glowing pearls,
now filled the pretty flowerlets' eyes
like tears that cried over their own disgrace.
After I had teased her to my heart's content,
she gently begged me to be patient.
55 Then I asked her for her changeling child,
and she immediately gave him to me, sending her fairy
to take him to my chamber in fairyland.
Now that I have the boy, I will remove
this hateful error in her vision.
60 And you, gentle Puck, remove this ass's head

From off the head of this Athenian swain,
That, he awaking when the other do,
May all to Athens back again repair,
And think no more of this night's accidents
65 But as the fierce vexation of a dream.
But first I will release the fairy queen.
[*Touching her eyes.*]
Be as thou wast wont to be;
See as thou wast wont to see:
Dian's bud o'er Cupid's flower
70 Hath such force and blessed power.
Now, my Titania; wake you, my sweet queen.

TITANIA
My Oberon! what visions have I seen!
Methought I was enamour'd of an ass.

OBERON
There lies your love.

TITANIA
75 How came these things to pass?
O, how mine eyes do loathe his visage now!

OBERON
Silence awhile. Robin, take off this head.
Titania, music call; and strike more dead
Than common sleep of all these five the sense.

TITANIA
80 Music, ho! music, such as charmeth sleep!
[*Music, still.*]

ROBIN GOODFELLOW
Now, when thou wak'st, with thine own fool's eyes peep.

OBERON
Sound, music! Come, my queen, take hands with me,
And rock the ground whereon these sleepers be.
Now thou and I are new in amity
85 And will to-morrow midnight solemnly
Dance in Duke Theseus' house triumphantly

---

69 *Dian's bud* a flower from a special tree believed to keep one chaste like the virgin goddess Diana.

from the head of this Athenian lover
so that when he awakes at the same time as the others,
they can all go back to Athens,
and think no more about the events of this night
65 except as the disturbance of a bad dream.
But first I will release the fairy queen.
To TITANIA.
Be as you used to be.
See as you used to see.
Over Cupid's flower, Diana's flower
70 Has force and blessed power.
Now, my Titania, awake, my sweet queen!

TITANIA
My Oberon, I have dreamed such strange things!
I thought I was in love with an ass.

OBERON
There lies your love.

TITANIA
75 How did this happen?
O, how my eyes hate his face now.

OBERON
Be quiet now. Robin, take off this ass's head.
Titania, call for music and put these five
into an uncommonly deep sleep.

TITANIA
80 Music! Bring music! Music that will charm them to sleep!
(Music is played.)

PUCK
Now when you awake, see with your own foolish eyes.

OBERON
Sound the music! Come, my queen, join hands,
and we'll rock the ground where these sleepers lie.
(They dance.)
Now you and I are renewed in love,
85 and tomorrow night, we will ceremoniously
dance in Duke Theseus' house in all our glory,

And bless it to all fair prosperity.
There shall the pairs of faithful lovers be
Wedded, with Theseus, all in jollity.

ROBIN GOODFELLOW

90 Fairy king, attend and mark;
I do hear the morning lark.

OBERON

Then, my queen, in silence sad
Trip we after the night's shade.
We the globe can compass soon,
95 Swifter than the wand'ring moon.

TITANIA

Come, my lord, and in our flight
Tell me how it came this night
That I sleeping here was found
With these mortals on the ground.
[*Exeunt. Horns winded within.*]

Enter THESEUS, HIPPOLYTA, EGEUS, *and all his train.*

THESEUS

100 Go, one of you, find out the forester,
For now our observation is perform'd,
And since we have the vaward of the day,
My love shall hear the music of my hounds.
Uncouple in the western valley, let them go.
105 Despatch, I say, and find the forester.
[*Exit an attendant.*]
We will, fair queen, up to the mountain's top
And mark the musical confusion
Of hounds and echo in conjunction.

HIPPOLYTA

I was with Hercules and Cadmus once,
110 When in a wood of Crete they bay'd the bear
With hounds of Sparta. Never did I hear

---

109 *Hercules and Cadmus* two heroes of Greek mythology. 110 *Crete* an island in th southeastern part of the Mediterranean Sea. 111 *Sparta* a city state in the Peloponnesia Peninsula.

and give them our blessings for a happy future.
There the pairs of faithful lovers will be
wedded, along with Theseus, in great merriment.

PUCK

90 Fairy king, listen.
I hear the morning lark.

OBERON

Then, my queen, with serious ceremony,
We'll follow the night, stepping light.
We can circle the world in a twinkling,
95 Swifter than the wandering moon.

TITANIA

Come, my lord, and during our flight,
Tell me how it came about tonight
That you found me sleeping here
100 On the ground with these human beings.
They exit.
A horn is heard and THESEUS *enters with* HIPPOLYTA, EGEUS, *and all of his train.*

THESEUS

100 Go, one of you, find the forester.
For now we've performed our May Day rites.
And since the day is just beginning,
you, my love, will hear the music of my hounds.
Let them loose in the western valley; let them go.
105 Go, I say, and find the forester.
An attendant exits.
Beautiful queen, we will go up to the mountain top,
and listen to the musical confusion of the sounds
of hounds and echoes mixed together.

HIPPOLYTA

I was with Hercules and Cadmus once
10 when in a wood of Crete they cornered a bear
with Spartan dogs. I have never heard

Such gallant chiding; for, besides the groves,
The skies, the fountains, every region near
Seem'd all one mutual cry. I never heard
115 So musical a discord, such sweet thunder.

THESEUS
My hounds are bred out of the Spartan kind,
So flew'd, so sanded, and their heads are hung
With ears that sweep away the morning dew;
Crook-knee'd, and dew-lapp'd like Thessalian bulls;
120 Slow in pursuit, but match'd in mouth like bells,
Each under each. A cry more tuneable
Was never holla'd to, nor cheer'd with horn,
In Crete, in Sparta, nor in Thessaly.
Judge when you hear. But, soft! what nymphs are these?

EGEUS
125 My lord, this is my daughter here asleep;
And this, Lysander; this Demetrius is;
This Helena, old Nedar's Helena.
I wonder of their being here together.

THESEUS
No doubt they rose up early to observe
130 The rite of May, and, hearing our intent,
Came here in grace of our solemnity.
But speak, Egeus; is not this the day
That Hermia should give answer of her choice?

EGEUS
It is, my lord.

THESEUS
135 Go, bid the huntsmen wake them with their horns.
[*Horns and shout within.* LYSANDER, DEMETRIUS, HELENA, *and* HERMIA *wake and start up.*]
Good morrow, friends. Saint Valentine is past;
Begin these wood-birds but to couple now?

LYSANDER
Pardon, my lord.

---

123 *Thessaly* a large area of ancient Greece. 136-37 *Saint Valentine . . . now?* Bird supposedly began mating on St. Valentine's Day, February 14.

such loud yowling. Besides the woods,
the skies, the fountains, and every place nearby
seemed to be ringing with the same sound. I never heard
115 such musical clamoring, such sweet thunder.

THESEUS
My hounds are bred from the Spartan breed.
They have the same sagging cheeks, the sandy color, and they have
ears so low that they sweep the dewy ground.
They have bent knees, and they have dewlaps like Thessalian bulls.
120 They are slow in pursuit, but their voices are matched like bells
of different tones. A more tuneful pack of hounds
was never yelled to or cheered with horns,
in Crete, in Sparta, or in Thessaly.
Judge for yourself when you hear. But, stop! Who are
these nymphs?

EGEUS
125 My lord, this is my daughter here asleep.
And this is Lysander. This is Demetrius.
This is Helena—old Nedar's Helena.
I wonder why they are here together.

THESEUS
No doubt they arose early to perform
130 the May Day rites, and hearing of our plans,
they came here to honor our ceremony.
But tell me, Egeus, isn't this the day
that Hermia must announce her choice?

EGEUS
It is, my lord.

THESEUS
35 Go, tell the hunters to wake them with their horns.
(A shout is heard offstage. Horns sound. The lovers all wake up.)
Good morning, friends. Saint Valentine is past.
Are these birds just starting to mate at this late date?

LYSANDER
I beg your pardon, my lord.

THESEUS

I pray you all, stand up.
140 I know you two are rival enemies;
How comes this gentle concord in the world,
That hatred is so far from jealousy
To sleep by hate and fear no enmity?

LYSANDER

My lord, I shall reply amazedly,
145 Half asleep, half waking; but as yet, I swear,
I cannot truly say how I came here.
But, as I think,—for truly would I speak,
And now I do bethink me, so it is,—
I came with Hermia hither. Our intent
150 Was to be gone from Athens, where we might,
Without the peril of the Athenian law—

EGEUS

Enough, enough, my lord; you have enough.
I beg the law, the law, upon his head.
They would have stol'n away; they would, Demetrius,
155 Thereby to have defeated you and me,
You of your wife, and me of my consent,
Of my consent that she should be your wife.

DEMETRIUS

My lord, fair Helen told me of their stealth,
Of this their purpose hither to this wood;
160 And I in fury hither follow'd them,
Fair Helena in fancy following me.
But, my good lord, I wot not by what power,—
But by some power it is,—my love to Hermia,
Melted as is the snow, seems to me now
165 As the remembrance of an idle gaud
Which in my childhood I did dote upon;
And all the faith, the virtue of my heart,
The object and the pleasure of mine eye,
Is only Helena. To her, my lord,
170 Was I betroth'd ere I saw Hermia;
But like a sickness did I loathe this food;

THESEUS

I beg you all, stand up.
140 I know you two young men are rivals in love,
so how does it happen that you are so at peace,
and your hatred is so far removed from suspicion
that you can sleep by one you hate and fear no harm?

LYSANDER

My lord, I will give you a confused reply
145 since I am half asleep and half awake. But right now, I swear,
I cannot truthfully say how I got here.
But, I think—for I want to be honest,
and now that I remember, this seems to be the case—
I came here with Hermia. It was our intention
150 to get away from Athens, to go somewhere where we might
escape Athenian law—

EGEUS

Enough! Enough, my lord! You have heard enough.
I beg you bring down the law upon his head.
They have run away—they would have, Demetrius!
155 They would have deprived you and me,
you of your wife and me of my consent—
my consent that she should be your wife.

DEMETRIUS

My lord, lovely Helen told me of their flight
and of their intention to come here to this woods.
160 And I, in a fury, followed them here,
with lovely Helena following me out of love.
But, my good lord, I don't know what power
—but some power has done it—my love for Hermia
has melted like the snow and now seems
165 like the memory of a worthless trinket
which I used to adore in my childhood.
Now all the faith and power of my heart
and the object and pleasure of my eyes
is Helena alone. I was engaged
170 to her before I saw Hermia.
But, like a sick person, I hated this food. (*Points to Helena.*)

But, as in health, come to my natural taste,
Now I do wish it, love it, long for it,
And will for evermore be true to it.

THESEUS
175 Fair lovers, you are fortunately met;
Of this discourse we more will hear anon.
Egeus, I will overbear your will;
For in the temple, by and by, with us
These couples shall eternally be knit.
180 And, for the morning now is something worn,
Our purpos'd hunting shall be set aside.
Away with us to Athens; three and three,
We'll hold a feast in great solemnity.
Come, Hippolyta.
[*Exeunt* THESEUS, HIPPOLYTA, EGEUS, *and train.*]

DEMETRIUS
185 These things seem small and undistinguishable,
Like far-off mountains turned into clouds.

HERMIA
Methinks I see these things with parted eye,
When every thing seems double.

HELENA
So methinks;
190 And I have found Demetrius like a jewel,
Mine own, and not mine own.

DEMETRIUS
But are you sure
That we are now awake? It seems to me
That yet we sleep, we dream. Do not you think
195 The Duke was here, and bid us follow him?

HERMIA
Yea; and my father.

HELENA
And Hippolyta.

But now, like a healthy man my natural taste has reformed.
Now, I want her, love her, long for her,
and I will always be true to her.

THESEUS
175 Beautiful lovers, you have happily reconciled.
I want to hear more about your story as soon as possible.
Egeus, I will overrule your wishes
because shortly, in the temple along with us,
these couples will be eternally joined in marriage.
180 Since the morning is somewhat spent,
our intended hunt will be postponed.
Let's all go to Athens! Three men and three women—
we'll hold a wedding feast with great ceremony.
Come, Hippolyta.
THESEUS, HIPPOLYTA, EGEUS, *and their followers all exit.*

DEMETRIUS
185 Everything seems small and undistinguishable,
like far-off mountains disappearing among clouds.

HERMIA
I think I see everything out of focus,
as when everything seems doubled.

HELENA
I think so, too.
190 And I have found Demetrius, like finding a jewel.
He is mine, and yet not mine.

DEMETRIUS
Are you sure
that we are awake? It seems to me
that we are still asleep, still dreaming. Don't you think
195 the duke was here, and he told us to follow him?

HERMIA
Yes, and my father.

HELENA
And Hippolyta.

LYSANDER
And he did bid us follow to the temple.

DEMETRIUS
Why, then, we are awake. Let's follow him;
200 And by the way let us recount our dreams.
[*Exeunt lovers.*]

BOTTOM
[*Awaking.*] When my cue comes, call me, and I will answer. My next is, "Most fair Pyramus." Heigh-ho! Peter Quince! Flute, the bellows-mender! Snout, the tinker! Starveling! God's my life, stolen hence, and left me asleep! I have had a most rare vision. 205 I have had a dream, past the wit of man to say what dream it was. Man is but an ass, if he go about to expound this dream. Methought I was—there is no man can tell what. Methought I was,—and methought I had,—but man is but a patch'd fool, if he will offer to say what methought I had. The eye of man hath 210 not heard, the ear of man hath not seen, man's hand is not able to taste, his tongue to conceive, nor his heart to report, what my dream was. I will get Peter Quince to write a ballad of this dream. It shall be called "Bottom's Dream," because it hath no bottom; and I will sing it in the latter end of a play, before the Duke; 215 peradventure, to make it the more gracious, I shall sing it at her death.
[*Exit.*]

Act IV, Scene ii: [*Athens. Quince's house.*] *Enter* QUINCE, FLUTE, SNOUT, *and* STARVELING.

QUINCE
Have you sent to Bottom's house? Is he come home yet?

STARVELING
He cannot be heard of. Out of doubt he is transported.

FLUTE
If he come not, then the play is marr'd. It goes not forward, doth it?

---

208 *patch'd fool* dressed like a professional fool (jester).

LYSANDER
And he told us to follow him to the temple.

DEMETRIUS
Well then, we are awake. Let's follow him,
200 and along the way, we'll tell each other our dreams.
They exit.

BOTTOM *(Awakening)*
When my cue comes, call me, and I will answer. My
next line is, "Most beautiful Pyramus." Hello! Peter Quince! Flute,
the bellows mender! Snout, the tinker! Starveling! God bless me!
They've snuck away and left me asleep! I've had a most
unusual dream.
205 I've had a dream—it's beyond the power of human reason to
say what kind of dream it
was. A man would be an ass if he tried to explain this dream.
I thought I was—there is no one who can tell what. I thought I
was—and I thought I had—but a man would be just a fool
dressed in motley if
he would try to say what I thought had happened. The eye of
man has
210 not heard, the ear of man has not seen, man's hand isn't able
to taste, his tongue can't imagine, or his heart explain what my
dream was about. I will get Peter Quince to write a ballad
about this dream.
It will be called "Bottom's Dream" because it doesn't have
a bottom.
And I will sing it at the end of the play, before the duke.
215 Perhaps to make it all the more gracious, I will sing it at Thisby's
death.
He exits.

Act IV, Scene ii: Athens. Quince's House. Enter QUINCE,
FLUTE, SNOUT, *and* STARVELING.

QUINCE
Have you sent someone to Bottom's house? Has he come home yet?

STARVELING
No one has heard a word about him. No doubt he has been
magically carried off.

FLUTE
If he doesn't come, then the play is ruined. The play won't go on,
will it?

QUINCE

5 It is not possible. You have not a man in all Athens able to discharge Pyramus but he.

FLUTE

No, he hath simply the best wit of any handicraft man in Athens.

SNOUT

Yea, and the best person too; and he is a very paramour for a sweet voice.

FLUTE

10 You must say "paragon"; a paramour is, God bless us, a thing of naught.

Enter SNUG.

SNUG

Masters, the Duke is coming from the temple, and there is two or three lords and ladies more married. If our sport had gone forward, we had all been made men.

FLUTE

15 O sweet bully Bottom! Thus hath he lost sixpence a day during his life; he could not have 'scaped sixpence a day. An the Duke had not given him sixpence a day for playing Pyramus, I'll be hang'd. He would have deserved it. Sixpence a day in Pyramus, or nothing.

Enter BOTTOM.

BOTTOM

20 Where are these lads? Where are these hearts?

QUINCE

Bottom! O most courageous day! O most happy hour!

BOTTOM

Masters, I am to discourse wonders, but ask me not what; for if I tell you, I am no true Athenian. I will tell you everything right as it fell out.

QUINCE

25 Let us hear, sweet Bottom.

QUINCE

5 It would be impossible. There's not a man in all Athens able to portray Pyramus except him.

FLUTE

You're right. He simply has the best mind of any craftsman in Athens.

SNOUT

Yes, and he's the best appearance, too. And he's a real paramour with that sweet voice of his.

FLUTE

10 You mean "paragon." A "paramour" is—God bless us—a wicked thing.

Enter SNUG.

SNUG

Gentlemen, the duke is coming from the temple, and with him are two or three more lords and ladies who have been married. If our play had gone on, we'd all have made our fortunes.

FLUTE

15 O sweet, grand Bottom! He's lost a pension of sixpence a day for life. He could not have escaped being given a sixpence a day. If the duke hadn't given him sixpence a day for playing Pyramus, I'll be hanged! He would have deserved it. Either sixpence a day for Pyramus or nothing!

Enter BOTTOM.

BOTTOM

20 Where are my chums? Where are my hearties?

QUINCE

Bottom! O what a splendid day! O what a happy hour!

BOTTOM

Gentlemen, I have wonders to tell, but don't ask me what. If I tell you, I'm not a true Athenian. I will tell you everything, just as it came about.

QUINCE

25 Tell us, sweet Bottom.

BOTTOM

Not a word of me. All that I will tell you is, that the Duke hat
dined. Get your apparel together, good strings to your beard
new ribbons to your pumps; meet presently at the palace; ever
man look o'er his part; for the short and the long is, our pla
30 is preferr'd. In any case, let Thisby have clean linen; and let nc
him that plays the lion pare his nails, for they shall hang out fc
the lion's claws. And, most dear actors, eat no onions nor garli
for we are to utter sweet breath; and I do not doubt but to hea
them say, it is a sweet comedy. No more words; away! go, away

[*Exeunt.*]

Act V, Scene i: [*Athens. The palace of Theseus.*] *Enter* THESEUS, HIPPOLYTA, PHILOSTRATE, *Lords, and Attendants.*

HIPPOLYTA

'Tis strange, my Theseus, that these lovers speak of.

THESEUS

More strange than true; I never may believe
These antique fables, nor these fairy toys.
Lovers and madmen have such seething brains,
5 Such shaping fantasies, that apprehend
More than cool reason ever comprehends.
The lunatic, the lover, and the poet
Are of imagination all compact.
One sees more devils than vast hell can hold;
10 That is, the madman. The lover, all as frantic,
See Helen's beauty in a brow of Egypt.
The poet's eye, in a fine frenzy rolling,
Doth glance from heaven to earth, from earth to heaven;
And as imagination bodies forth
15 The forms of things unknown, the poet's pen
Turns them to shapes and gives to airy nothing
A local habitation and a name.
Such tricks hath strong imagination,

---

11 *Helen's . . . Egypt* Helen of Troy was a renowned Greek beauty. To the Elizabetha who valued a pale complexion, the dark face of a gypsy would be a marked contrast an ideal beauty.

BOTTOM

Not a word from me. All that I will tell you is that the duke has eaten. Get your clothes together and good strings for your beards and new ribbons for your shoes. Meet me at the palace at once. Every one
of you must review his part, for the long and short of it is, our play
30 has been recommended. Be sure that Thisby has clean clothes, and don't let
the one who plays the lion cut his nails because they should hang out like
lion's claws. And, my dear actors, don't eat any onions or garlic,
for we are to utter sweet words, and I'm sure
they'll say it's a sweet comedy. Not another word! Away! Go!

They exit.

Act V, Scene i: Athens. The palace of Theseus. Enter THESEUS, HIPPOLYTA, PHILOSTRATE, *Lords, and attendants.*

HIPPOLYTA

These lovers speak of strange things, my Theseus.

THESEUS

It is more strange than true. I can never believe
these fanciful fables or these fairy fantasies.
Lovers and madmen have seething brains
5 and creative imaginations that conceive
more than cool reason ever comprehends.
The lunatic, the lover, and the poet
are entirely constructed out of imagination.
One of them sees more devils than far-reaching hell can hold—
10 that one is the madman. The lover, just as frantic,
sees beauty equal to Helen's in a gypsy's face.
The poet's eye, rolling in great frenzy,
glances from heaven to earth and from earth to heaven.
And as imagination calls into being
15 the forms of strange things, the poet's pen
forms them into shapes and gives these airy nothings
a home and a name.
A strong imagination is filled with such tricks

That, if it would but apprehend some joy,
20 It comprehends some bringer of that joy;
Or in the night, imagining some fear,
How easy is a bush suppos'd a bear!

HIPPOLYTA
But all the story of the night told over,
And all their minds transfigur'd so together,
25 More witnesseth than fancy's images,
And grows to something of great constancy;
But, howsoever, strange and admirable.
Enter lovers, LYSANDER, DEMETRIUS, HERMIA, *and* HELENA.

THESEUS
Here come the lovers, full of joy and mirth.
Joy, gentle friends! joy and fresh days of love
30 Accompany your hearts!

LYSANDER
More than to us
Wait in your royal walks, your board, your bed!

THESEUS
Come now; what masques, what dances shall we have,
To wear away this long age of three hours
35 Between our after-supper and bed-time?
Where is our usual manager of mirth?
What revels are in hand? Is there no play
To ease the anguish of a torturing hour?
Call Philostrate.

PHILOSTRATE
40 Here, mighty Theseus.

THESEUS
Say, what abridgement have you for this evening?
What masque? what music? How shall we beguile
The lazy time, if not with some delight?

---

19 *it* the imagination. 33 *masque* a form of entertainment consisting of dance and theatrics where the performers wore masks.

that if it wants to experience some joy,
20 it will dream of someone to bring that joy.
Or in the night, when one is imagining fearful things,
how easily imagination turns a bush into a bear!

HIPPOLYTA
But when the whole story of the night was told,
and all of their minds proved to be affected by the same delusion,
25 it emerges there is more to this than imagination's images
and it becomes a story of great consistency.
At any rate, it is strange and wonderful.
Enter the lovers: LYSANDER, DEMETRIUS, HERMIA, *and* HELENA.

THESEUS
Here come the lovers, full of joy and mirth.
Joy to you, gentle friends. May joy and the fresh days of love
30 stay in your hearts.

LYSANDER
May more joy than awaits us
wait for you in your royal walks, your table, and your bed!

THESEUS
Come, what masques and dances shall we have
to wear away the long three hours
35 between dessert and bedtime?
Where is our regular manager of entertainment?
What celebrations are on hand? Is there no play
to ease the anguish of enduring a torturing hour?
Call Philostrate.

PHILOSTRATE
40 I am here, mighty Theseus.

THESEUS
Tell me, what pastime do you have for this evening?
What masque? What music? How shall we while away
the lazy time if not with some delightful entertainment?

PHILOSTRATE

There is a brief how many sports are ripe.
45 Make choice of which your Highness will see first.
[*Giving a paper.*]

THESEUS

[*Reads.*] "The battle with the Centaurs, to be sung
By an Athenian eunuch to the harp."
We'll none of that: that have I told my love,
In glory of my kinsman Hercules.
50 "The riot of the tipsy Bacchanals,
Tearing the Thracian singer in their rage."
That is an old device; and it was play'd
When I from Thebes came last a conqueror.
"The thrice three Muses mourning for the death
55 Of Learning, late deceas'd in beggary."
That is some satire, keen and critical,
Not sorting with a nuptial ceremony.
"A tedious brief scene of young Pyramus
And his love Thisbe; very tragical mirth."
60 Merry and tragical! Tedious and brief!
That is, hot ice and wondrous strange snow.
How shall we find the concord of this discord?

PHILOSTRATE

A play there is, my lord, some ten words long,
Which is as brief as I have known a play;
65 But by ten words, my lord, it is too long,
Which makes it tedious; for in all the play
There is not one word apt, one player fitted.
And tragical, my noble lord, it is;
For Pyramus therein doth kill himself.
70 Which, when I saw rehears'd, I must confess,
Made mine eyes water; but more merry tears
The passion of loud laughter never shed.

THESEUS

What are they that do play it?

---

46 *battle with the Centaurs* probably refers to the Greek hero Hercules' battle with th Centaurs (creatures who were half man, half horse) while he was completing his famou Twelve Labors. 51 *Thracian singer* is Orpheus, whose musical ability impressed men an

PHILOSTRATE

Here is a list of the many delights that are ready.
45 Choose which one you will see first, your highness.
(He gives Theseus a paper.)

THESEUS *(Reads)*

"The battle with the centaurs, to be sung
by an Athenian eunuch accompanied by a harp."
We'll have none of that. I have already told my love that story
to honor my kinsman Hercules.
50 *(Reads)* "The riot of the tipsy Bacchanals
as they tear apart the singer Orpheus in their rage."
That is an old show and it was played
when I last came from Thebes as a conqueror.
(Reads) "The nine Muses mourning for the death
55 of Learning, who recently died a beggar."
That is a satire, sharp and critical.
It is not suited to a wedding ceremony.
(Reads) "A tedious, brief scene about young Pyramus
and his lover Thisby—a very tragic comedy."
60 Merry and tragic? Tedious and brief?
That is like hot ice and wonderfully strange snow.
How shall we find agreement between these contradictions?

PHILOSTRATE

It is a play, my lord, about ten words long,
which is as short a play as I have ever seen.
65 But even with just ten words, my lord, it is too long
and that's why it's tedious. For in all that play,
there is not one suitable word or one well-cast actor.
And it's tragic, my lord,
Pyramus does kill himself—
70 which, when I saw the play rehearsed, I must confess,
brought tears to my eyes. But merrier tears
were never shed out of amusement.

THESEUS

Who are the people who perform this play?

---

gods alike. Orpheus was killed by frenzied, drunken devotees of the god of wine, Bacchus.
54 *Muses* Greek goddesses of the arts.

PHILOSTRATE
Hard-handed men that work in Athens here,
75 Which never labour'd in their minds till now,
And now have toil'd their unbreath'd memories
With this same play, against your nuptial.

THESEUS
And we will hear it.

PHILOSTRATE
No, my noble lord;
80 It is not for you. I have heard it over,
And it is nothing, nothing in the world;
Unless you can find sport in their intents,
Extremely stretch'd and conn'd with cruel pain,
To do you service.

THESEUS
85 I will hear that play;
For never anything can be amiss,
When simpleness and duty tender it.
Go, bring them in; and take your places, ladies.
[*Exit* PHILOSTRATE.]

HIPPOLYTA
I love not to see wretchedness o'er-charged,
90 And duty in his service perishing.

THESEUS
Why, gentle sweet, you shall see no such thing.

HIPPOLYTA
He says they can do nothing in this kind.

THESEUS
The kinder we, to give them thanks for nothing.
Our sport shall be to take what they mistake;
95 And what poor duty cannot do, noble respect
Takes it in might, not merit.
Where I have come, great clerks have purposed
To greet me with premeditated welcomes;
Where I have seen them shiver and look pale,

PHILOSTRATE
They are laborers who work here in Athens,
75 but they never labored with their minds until now.
Now they are laboring with their unexercised memories
over this play, prepared for your wedding.

THESEUS
And we will see it.

PHILOSTRATE
No, my noble lord.
80 It is not for you. I have seen it,
and it is nothing—nothing in the world—
unless you can find amusement in their efforts,
which are extremely strained, and their lines which have
been memorized with great pain
in order to serve you.

THESEUS
85 I will see their play,
for nothing can be wrong
when it is presented with simpleness and duty.
Go, bring them in. Take your places, ladies.
PHILOSTRATE *exits.*

HIPPOLYTA
I don't like to see poor people pushed beyond their limits
90 in order to do you service.

THESEUS
Why, my gentle sweet, you shall see no such thing.

HIPPOLYTA
He (Philostrate) says they can not act at all.

THESEUS
Then we are all the kinder for thanking them for nothing.
Our amusement will be in accepting their blunders.
95 And whatever poor service they cannot do, our noble minds
will value the effort they make, not their ability.
On my travels, I have met great scholars who intended
to greet me with prepared welcoming speeches.
And I have seen them shiver and turn pale,

100 Make periods in the midst of sentences,
Throttle their practis'd accent in their fears,
And in conclusion dumbly have broke off,
Not paying me a welcome. Trust me, sweet,
Out of this silence yet I pick'd a welcome;
105 And in the modesty of fearful duty
I read as much as from the rattling tongue
Of saucy and audacious eloquence.
Love, therefore, and tongue-ti'd simplicity
In least speak most, to my capacity.

Re-enter PHILOSTRATE.

PHILOSTRATE

110 So please your Grace, the Prologue is address'd.

THESEUS

Let him approach. [*Flourish of trumpets.*]

Enter QUINCE *for the* PROLOGUE.

PROLOGUE

If we offend, it is with our good will.
That you should think, we come not to offend,
But with good will. To show our simple skill,
115 That is the true beginning of our end.
Consider then we come but in despite.
We do not come as minding to content you,
Our true intent is. All for your delight
We are not here. That you should here repent you,
120 The actors are at hand, and by their show
You shall know all that you are like to know.

THESEUS

This fellow doth not stand upon points.

LYSANDER

He hath rid his prologue like a rough colt; he knows not the stop.
A good moral, my lord: it is not enough to speak, but to
125 speak true.

HIPPOLYTA

Indeed he hath play'd on this prologue like a child on a recorder;
a sound, but not in government.

---

110 *Prologue* introduces and explains a play. The player who gave these introductions was known as the prologue, too. 112, ff. *If we, . . .* Quince pauses in the wrong places throughout his speech, comically misreading his lines. 122 *stand upon points* is a pun

100 stop in the middle of sentences,
choke on their rehearsed speeches in their fear.
And, in conclusion, they silently broke off
without giving me a welcome. Trust me, sweet.
Out of their silence, I still picked out a welcome.
105 And in their shyness, caused by their respect for me,
I read as much as from a tongue wagging
with saucy and bold eloquence.
Therefore, love and tongue-tied modesty
speak the most when the least is said, as I see it.
Enter PHILOSTRATE.

PHILOSTRATE
110 If it please your grace, the prologue is ready.

THESEUS
Let him approach.
(There is a flourish of trumpets.)
THE PROLOGUE, QUINCE, *enters.*

PROLOGUE
If we offend you, we do it with the best of intentions.
You must believe that we have come not to offend,
But with good intentions. To show our simple skill,
115 That is the real reason we are here.
Consider this then, that we come in spite of that.
We did not come with the idea of pleasing you,
Our true intention is. For your pleasure,
We are not here. So that you shall repent,
120 The actors are ready. And from their performance,
You will learn everything, that you are likely to learn.

THESEUS
This fellow isn't one to worry about the finer points.

LYSANDER
He rode his prologue like a wild colt. He doesn't know
what a stop is.
A good moral, my lord is "It is not enough to speak, we
125 must speak correctly, too."

HIPPOLYTA
Indeed, he played on his prologue like a child plays on a flute—
a sound, but not under his control.

---

neaning both "careful about proper punctuation" and "fastidious." 123 *stop* another
oun, meaning both "to halt a horse" and "period."

THESEUS
His speech was like a tangled chain; nothing impaired, but all disordered. Who is next?

Enter with a trumpet before them, PYRAMUS *and* THISBE, WALL, MOONSHINE, *and* LION.

PROLOGUE
130 Gentles, perchance you wonder at this show;
But wonder on till truth make all things plain.
This man is Pyramus, if you would know;
This beauteous lady Thisby is certain.
This man, with lime and rough-cast, doth present
135 Wall, that vile Wall which did these lovers sunder;
And through Wall's chink, poor souls, they are content
To whisper. At the which let no man wonder.
This man, with lantern, dog, and bush of thorn,
Presenteth Moonshine; for, if you will know,
140 By moonshine did these lovers think no scorn
To meet at Ninus' tomb, there, there to woo.
This grisly breast, which Lion hight by name,
The trusty Thisby, coming first by night,
Did scare away, or rather did affright;
145 And, as she fled, her mantle she did fall,
Which Lion vile with bloody mouth did stain.
Anon comes Pyramus, sweet youth and tall,
And finds his trusty Thisby's mantle slain;
Whereat, with blade, with bloody blameful blade,
150 He bravely broach'd his boiling bloody breast;
And Thisby, tarrying in mulberry shade,
His dagger drew, and died. For all the rest,
Let Lion, Moonshine, Wall, and lovers twain
At large discourse, while here they do remain.

[*Exeunt* PROLOGUE, THISBE, LION, *and* MOONSHINE.]

THESEUS
155 I wonder if the lion be to speak.

DEMETRIUS
No wonder, my lord; one lion may, when many asses do.

THESEUS

His speech was like a tangled chain. Nothing was broken, but it was all in
disorder. Who is next?

A trumpet sounds. Enter PYRAMUS, THISBY, WALL, MOONSHINE, *and* LION.

PROLOGUE

130 Ladies and gentlemen, perhaps you are wondering about this display.
Well, wonder on until truth makes everything clear.
This man is Pyramus, if you want to know.
This beautiful lady is Thisby, indeed.
This man, covered with soil and plaster, represents
135 The wall—that horrible wall which separated these lovers.
And through a crack in the wall, poor souls, they are content
To whisper. None of you must be amazed by this.
This man with the lantern, dog, and thorn bush
Represents Moonshine. Because, if you would like to know,
140 These lovers are not ashamed to meet
By moonlight at Ninus' tomb to kiss and court.
This terrible beast which is called a lion,
Scares away the trusting Thisby who comes first that night,
Or rather, frightens her.
145 And as she runs away, she drops her cloak
Which the lion stains with his horrible bloody mouth.
Soon along comes Pyramus, a sweet, brave young man,
And finds his trusting Thisby's cloak destroyed.
When he sees this, with his sword—his bloody, deadly sword—
150 He bravely stabs his boiling, bloody breast.
Then Thisby, hiding in the dark shadows,
Drew his dagger and killed herself. As for all the rest,
Let Lion, Moonshine, Wall, and lovers together,
Tell you at length while they are here.

Exit PROLOGUE, THISBY, LION, *and* MOONSHINE.

THESEUS

155 I wonder if the lion will speak.

DEMETRIUS

It would not be a surprise, my lord. One lion might when so many asses do.

WALL
In this same interlude it doth befall
That I, one Snout by name, present a wall;
And such a wall, as I would have you think,
160 That had in it a crannied hole or chink,
Through which the lovers, Pyramus and Thisby,
Did whisper often very secretly.
This loam, this rough-cast, and this stone doth show
That I am that same wall; the truth is so;
165 And this the cranny is, right and sinister,
Through which the fearful lovers are to whisper.

THESEUS
Would you desire lime and hair to speak better?

DEMETRIUS
It is the wittiest partition that ever I heard discourse, my lord.
Enter PYRAMUS.

THESEUS
Pyramus draws near the wall. Silence!

PYRAMUS
170 O grim-look'd night! O night with hue black!
O night, which ever art when day is not!
O night, O night! alack, alack, alack,
I fear my Thisby's promise is forgot!
And thou, O wall, O sweet, O lovely wall,
175 That stand'st between her father's ground and mine!
Thou wall, O wall, O sweet and lovely wall,
Show me thy chink, to blink through with mine eyne!
[WALL *holds up his fingers.*]
Thanks, courteous wall; Jove shield thee well for this!
But what see I? No Thisby do I see.
180 O wicked wall, through whom I see no bliss!
Curs'd be thy stones for thus deceiving me!

THESEUS
The wall, methinks, being sensible, should curse again.

WALL

During this part, it happens
that I, Snout by name, represent a wall.
And it is such a wall, as would have you know,
160 that has a hole or crack in it
through which the lovers Pyramus and Thisby
often whispered, very secretly.
This soil, this plaster, and this stone show
that I am that very wall. It is the truth.
165 And this is the crack, which runs horizontally *(shows crack, with his fingers),*
through which the frightened lovers will whisper.

THESEUS

Could you want plaster and hair to speak any better?

DEMETRIUS

It is the most intelligent wall I ever heard speak, my lord.
Enter PYRAMUS.

THESEUS

Pyramus is nearing the wall. Silence!

PYRAMUS

70 O grim night! O night with such a black color!
O night, which is always here when day is not!
O night, O night! Alas, alas, alas,
I am afraid my Thisby has forgotten her promise.
And you, O wall, O sweet, O lovely wall,
75 You stand between her father's property and mine!
You wall, O wall, O sweet and lovely wall,
Show me your crack, so I can peer through it with my eyes.
The WALL *holds up his fingers.*
Thanks, courteous wall. May God protect you well for this!
But what do I see? I do not see Thisby.
80 O wicked wall, through whom I see no happiness,
May your stones be cursed for deceiving me like this!

THESEUS

I think the wall, having feelings, should curse in return.

PYRAMUS

No, in truth, sir, he should not. "Deceiving me" is Thisby's cue
She is to enter now, and I am to spy her through the wall. Yo
185 shall see it will fall pat as I told you. Yonder she comes.

Enter THISBE.

THISBE

O wall, full often hast thou heard my moans,
For parting my fair Pyramus and me!
My cherry lips have often kiss'd thy stones,
Thy stones with lime and hair knit up in thee.

PYRAMUS

190 I see a voice! Now will I to the chink,
To spy an I can hear my Thisby's face.
Thisby!

THISBE

My love, thou art my love, I think.

PYRAMUS

Think what thou wilt, I am thy lover's grace;
195 And, like Limander, am I trusty still.

THISBE

And I like Helen, till the Fates me kill.

PYRAMUS

Not Shafalus to Procrus was so true.

THISBE

As Shafalus to Procrus, I to you.

PYRAMUS

O, kiss me through the hole of this vile wall!

THISBE

200 I kiss the wall's hole, not your lips at all.

PYRAMUS

Wilt thou at Ninny's tomb meet me straightway?

THISBE

'Tide life, 'tide death, I come without delay.

[*Exeunt* PYRAMUS *and* THISBE.]

190-91 *see . . . face* Bottom is confusing his lines. 195 *Limander* Bottom means Leand
Leander swam the Hellespont every night to see Hero—not Helen. 197 *Shafalus* Anot
of Bottom's humorous mistakes. He really means Cephalus who was married to Procus. Cep
lus resisted Aurora and remained true to Procus. 201 *Ninny's tomb* Bottom means Nin

PYRAMUS

No, in truth, sir, he should not. "Deceiving me" is Thisby's cue.
She will enter now, and I will see her through the wall. You
185 will see it happen exactly the way I told you. There she comes.

Enter THISBY.

THISBY

O wall, so often you have heard my moans
Because you separate my beautiful Pyramus and me!
My cherry lips have often kissed your stones—
Your stones made up of plaster and hair.

PYRAMUS

190 I see a voice! Now I will go to the crack
To see if I can hear my Thisby's face.
Thisby!

THISBY

My love! You are my love, I think.

PYRAMUS

Think what you will, I am your gracious lover.
195 And, like Limander, I am still faithful.

THISBY

And I will be as faithful as Helen until the Fates kill me.

PYRAMUS

Not even Shafalus was as faithful to Procus.

THISBY

As true as Shafalus was to Procus, I am to you.

PYRAMUS

O kiss me through the hole of this horrid wall!

THISBY

200 I can only kiss the wall's hole, not your lips at all.

PYRAMUS

Will you meet me right away at Ninny's tomb?

THISBY

Let life or death come, I will meet you without delay.

PYRAMUS *and* THISBY *exit.*

WALL
Thus have I, Wall, my part discharged so;
And, being done, thus Wall away doth go.
[*Exit.*]

THESEUS
205 Now is the moon used between the two neighbours.

DEMETRIUS
No remedy, my lord, when walls are so wilful to hear withou
warning.

HIPPOLYTA
This is the silliest stuff that ever I heard.

THESEUS
The best in this kind are but shadows; and the worst are no worse
210 if imagination amend them.

HIPPOLYTA
It must be your imagination then, and not theirs.

THESEUS
If we imagine no worse of them than they of themselves, the
may pass for excellent men. Here come two noble beasts in,
man and a lion.
Enter LION *and* MOONSHINE.

LION
215 You, ladies, you, whose gentle hearts do fear
The smallest monstrous mouse that creeps on floor,
May now perchance both quake and tremble here,
When lion rough in wildest rage doth roar.
Then know that I, as Snug the joiner, am
220 A lion fell, nor else no lion's dam;
For, if I should as lion come in strife
Into this place, 'twere pity on my life.

THESEUS
A very gentle beast, and of a good conscience.

DEMETRIUS
The very best at a beast, my lord, that e'er I saw.

---

205 *moon used* a confusing phrase that is often changed to "mural down" to make mo
sense.

WALL
Now I, Wall, have finished performing my part.
And since I am done, Wall will go away.
He exits.

THESEUS
205 Now the wall is down between the two neighbors.

DEMETRIUS
This doesn't help the situation, my lord, when walls are
so ready to listen without
warning others of mischief.

HIPPOLYTA
This is the silliest stuff I have ever heard.

THESEUS
Even the best plays are merely shadows. And the worst are no worse
210 if imagination comes to their aid.

HIPPOLYTA
Then it must be the imagination you supply, and not theirs.

THESEUS
If we imagine no worse of them than they think of themselves, they
may pass for excellent men. Here come two noble beasts, a
man and a lion.
Enter LION *and* MOONSHINE.

LION
215 You ladies, you whose gentle hearts fear
The smallest monstrous mouse that crawls on the floor,
May now perhaps shake and tremble here
When a rough lion roars in wildest rage.
So you must know that I am Snug the joiner—
220 Only the skin of a lion—not even a lioness.
For, if I should come as an angry lion
Into this place, it would mean my head.

THESEUS
He's a very polite beast, and has a good conscience.

DEMETRIUS
He is the very best beast, my lord, that I have ever seen.

LYSANDER

225 This lion is a very fox for his valour.

THESEUS

True; and a goose for his discretion.

DEMETRIUS

Not so, my lord; for his valour cannot carry his discretion, and the fox carries the goose.

THESEUS

His discretion, I am sure, cannot carry his valour; for the goose

230 carries not the fox. It is well; leave it to his discretion, and let us hearken to the moon.

MOONSHINE

This lantern doth the horned moon present;—

DEMETRIUS

He should have worn the horns on his head.

THESEUS

He is no crescent, and his horns are invisible within the

235 circumference.

MOONSHINE

This lantern doth the horned moon present;
Myself the man i' th' moon do seem to be.

THESEUS

This is the greatest error of all the rest. The man should be put into the lantern. How is it else the man i' th' moon?

DEMETRIUS

240 He dares not come there for the candle; for, you see, it is already in snuff.

HIPPOLYTA

I am aweary of this moon. Would he would change!

THESEUS

It appears, by his small light of discretion, that he is in the wane; but yet, in courtesy, in all reason, we must stay the time.

LYSANDER

245 Proceed, Moon.

---

233 *horns on his head* is a joke about a cuckold (a man whose wife is cheating on him) who has horns. 241 *in snuff* means both "offended" and "in need of snuffing."

LYSANDER

225 This lion is more foxy than he is brave.

THESEUS

True; and he is a goose in his discretion.

DEMETRIUS

No, my lord, because his bravery will never carry away his discretion, and
the fox carries away the goose.

THESEUS

I am sure his discretion, cannot take away his courage because the goose
230 does not carry away the fox. That is as it should be. Leave it to his discretion, and let
us listen to the moon.

MOONSHINE

This lantern represents the horned moon—

DEMETRIUS

He should have worn the horns on his own head.

THESEUS

He is not a crescent moon. His horns are invisible within the
235 circle of the full moon.

MOONSHINE

This lantern represents the horned moon.
I am supposed to be the man in the moon.

THESEUS

This is a greater mistake than all the rest. The man should be
inside the lantern. How else can he be the man in the moon?

DEMETRIUS

240 He does not dare go there on account of the candle, because, you see, it already
needs snuffing.

HIPPOLYTA

I am tired of this moon. I wish he would change!

THESEUS

It appears, judging by his dim intelligence, that he is waning.
Yet, out of courtesy and in all reason, we must wait him out.

LYSANDER

245 Go on, Moon.

MOONSHINE
All that I have to say, is, to tell you that the lantern is the moon; I, the man i' th' moon; this thorn-bush, my thorn-bush; and this dog, my dog.

DEMETRIUS
Why, all these should be in the lantern; for all these are in the
250 moon. But, silence! here comes Thisbe.
Re-enter THISBE.

THISBE
This is old Ninny's tomb. Where is my love?

LION
[*Roaring.*] Oh—
[THISBE *runs off.*]

DEMETRIUS
Well roar'd, Lion.

THESEUS
Well run, Thisbe.

HIPPOLYTA
255 Well shone, Moon. Truly, the moon shines with a good grace
[*The* LION *shakes* THISBE'S *mantle and exit.*]

THESEUS
Well mous'd, Lion.
Re-enter PYRAMUS.

DEMETRIUS
And then came Pyramus.

LYSANDER
And so the lion vanish'd.

PYRAMUS
Sweet Moon, I thank thee for thy sunny beams;
260 I thank thee, Moon, for shining now so bright;
For, by thy gracious, golden, glittering gleams,
I trust to take of truest Thisby sight.
But stay, O spite!
But mark, poor knight,

MOONSHINE
All I have to say is to tell you that the lantern is the moon.
I am the man in the moon. This thornbush is my thornbush, and this
dog is my dog.

DEMETRIUS
Why, all of these should be in the lantern, because all of these are in the
250 moon. But silence! Here comes Thisby.
Re-enter THISBY.

THISBY
This is old Ninny's tomb. Where is my love?

LION
O!
The LION *roars and* THISBY *runs off.*

DEMETRIUS
Well roared, Lion!

THESEUS
Well run, Thisby!

HIPPOLYTA
255 Well shone, Moon! Truly, the moon shines very graciously.
The LION *shakes Thisby's cloak and exits.*

THESEUS
Well shaken, Lion!
Re-enter PYRAMUS.

DEMETRIUS
And now comes Pyramus.

LYSANDER
And the Lion has disappeared.

PYRAMUS
Sweet Moon, I thank you for your sunny beams.
260 I thank you, Moon, for shining so bright.
For, by your gracious, golden, glittering gleams,
I hope to catch sight of my loyal Thisby.
But wait! O trouble!
But what is this, poor knight?

265 What dreadful dole is here!
Eyes, do you see?
How can it be?
O dainty duck! O dear!
Thy mantle good,
270 What, stain'd with blood!
Approach, ye Furies fell!
O Fates, come, come,
Cut thread and thrum;
Quail, crush, conclude, and quell!

THESEUS

275 This passion, and the death of a dear friend, would go near to make a man look sad.

HIPPOLYTA

Beshrew my heart, but I pity the man.

PYRAMUS

O wherefore Nature, didst thou lions frame?
Since lion vile hath here deflow'r'd my dear;
280 Which is—no, no—which was the fairest dame
That liv'd, that lov'd, that lik'd, that look'd with cheer.
Come, tears, confound;
Out, sword, and wound
The pap of Pyramus;
285 Ay, that left pap,
Where heart doth hop.
[*Stabs himself.*]
Thus die I, thus, thus, thus.
Now am I dead,
Now am I fled;
290 My soul is in the sky.
Tongue, lose thy light;
Moon, take thy flight.
[*Exit* MOONSHINE.]
Now die, die, die, die, die.
[*Dies.*]

---

271 *Furies* three deities who pursued and punished human wrongdoers.

265 What sorrowful thing is this?
Eyes, do you see?
How can it be?
O dainty duck! O dear!
Your good cloak.
270 Is this, stained with blood?
Come here, you dreadful Furies!
Come, come, you Fates!
End it all.
Overpower, crush, end, and kill!

THESEUS
275 All this grief and the death of a dear friend would almost make a man look sad.

HIPPOLYTA
Curse my heart, but I pity the man.

PYRAMUS
Why, O Nature, did you create lions?
A vile lion has here destroyed my love.
280 She is—no!—she was the loveliest girl
Who ever lived, who loved, who liked, who looked with a face.
Come, tears, kill me!
Out, sword, and wound
The breast of Pyramus.
285 Yes, the left breast
Where the heart beats.
(Stabs himself.)
So I die—thus, thus, thus.
Now I am dead.
Now I am gone.
290 My soul is in the sky.
Tongue, lose your speech.
Moon, fly away.
MOONSHINE *exits.*
Now—die, die, die, die, die.
(He dies.)

DEMETRIUS

No die, but an ace, for him; for he is but one.

LYSANDER

295 Less than an ace, man, for he is dead; he is nothing.

THESEUS

With the help of a surgeon he might yet recover, and yet prove an ass.

HIPPOLYTA

How chance Moonshine is gone before Thisbe comes back and finds her lover?

Re-enter THISBE.

THESEUS

300 She will find him by starlight. Here she comes; and her passion ends the play.

HIPPOLYTA

Methinks she should not use a long one for such a Pyramus. I hope she will be brief.

DEMETRIUS

A mote will turn the balance, which Pyramus, which Thisbe, is

305 the better; he for a man, God warrant us; she for a woman, God bless us.

LYSANDER

She hath spied him already with those sweet eyes.

DEMETRIUS

And thus she moans, *videlicet:*—

THISBE

Asleep, my love?

310 What, dead, my dove?

O Pyramus, arise!

Speak, speak! Quite dumb?

Dead, dead? A tomb

Must cover thy sweet eyes.

315 These lily lips,

This cherry nose,

These yellow cowslip cheeks,

315, ff. *lily lips* . . . Flute makes a humorous jumble of his speech. "Cherry lips," "yellow cowslip hair," etc., would be more appropriate.

DEMETRIUS
Not even a single die for him, but a one spot, for he is just one.

LYSANDER
295 He's less than a one spot, man, because he's dead; he's nothing.

THESEUS
With the help of a surgeon, he might still recover, and prove himself an ass still.

HIPPOLYTA
How can it be that Moonshine is gone before Thisby comes back and
finds her lover?

THISBY *enters.*

THESEUS
300 She will find him by starlight. Here she comes. Her passionate speech
ends the play.

HIPPOLYTA
I think she should not make a long speech for such a Pyramus as this. I
hope she will be brief.

DEMETRIUS
A speck would tip the scales whether Pyramus or Thisby is
305 better. He as a man, God save us! Or she as a woman, God bless us!

LYSANDER
She already has spied him with those sweet eyes.

DEMETRIUS
And so she moans, as follows:

THISBY
Asleep, my love?
310 What? Dead, my dove?
O Pyramus, arise!
Speak, speak! Completely mute?
Dead, dear? A tomb
Must cover your sweet eyes.
315 These lily lips,
This cherry nose,
These yellow cowslip cheeks,

Are gone, are gone!
Lovers, make moan.
320 His eyes were green as leeks.
O Sisters Three,
Come, come to me,
With hands as pale as milk;
Lay them in gore,
325 Since you have shore
With shears his thread of silk.
Tongue, not a word!
Come, trusty sword;
Come, blade, my breast imbrue!
[*Stabs herself.*]
330 And, farewell, friends;
Thus, Thisby ends.
Adieu, adieu, adieu.
[*Dies.*]

THESEUS
Moonshine and Lion are left to bury the dead.

DEMETRIUS
Ay, and Wall too.

BOTTOM
335 [*Starting up.*] No, I assure you; the wall is down that parted thei fathers. Will it please you to see the epilogue, or to hear Bergomask dance between two of our company?

THESEUS
No epilogue, I pray you; for your play needs no excuse. Neve excuse; for when the players are all dead, there need none to b
340 blamed. Marry, if he that writ it had played Pyramus and hang' himself in Thisbe's garter, it would have been a fine tragedy; an so it is, truly; and very notably discharg'd. But, come, you Bergomask; let your epilogue alone.
[*A dance.*]
The iron tongue of midnight hath told twelve.
345 Lovers, to bed; 'tis almost fairy time.
I fear we shall out-sleep the coming morn

320 *leeks* green onions. 321 *Sisters Three* the Furies. 337 *Bergomask dance* a rusti dance named for the country people of Bergamo, Italy.

Are gone, are gone!
Lovers, you must moan.
320 His eyes were as green as leeks.
O you three sisters of Fate.
Come, come to me,
With hands as white as milk.
Dip them in blood,
325 Since you have cut
With shears his thread of silk.
Tongue, don't say a word!
Come, trusty sword;
Come, blade, stain my breast with blood.
(She stabs herself.)
330 So goodbye friends.
This is the way Thisby ends.
Adieu, adieu, adieu.
(She dies.)

THESEUS
Moonshine and Lion are left to bury the dead.

DEMETRIUS
Yes, and Wall, too.

BOTTOM *(Starting to get up)*
335 No, I assure you, the wall is down that separated their fathers. Would you like to see the epilogue or hear a Bergomask dance by two men of our company?

THESEUS
No epilogue, I beg you, for your play needs no explanations. Never explain because when the actors are all dead, there is no one to be
340 blamed. Indeed, if the author had played Pyramus and hanged himself by Thisby's garter, it would have been a fine tragedy. And so it is, truly, and very remarkably presented. But, come, your dance. Forget your epilogue.
(The actors dance.)
The iron bell has struck twelve.
345 Lovers, go to bed; it is almost fairy time.
I am afraid we will outsleep the coming morning,

As much as we this night have overwatch'd.
This palpable-gross play hath well beguil'd
The heavy gait of night. Sweet friends, to bed.
350 A fortnight hold we this solemnity
In nightly revels and new jollity.
[*Exeunt.*]

Enter ROBIN GOODFELLOW.

ROBIN GOODFELLOW
Now the hungry lion roars,
And the wolf behowls the moon;
Whilst the heavy ploughman snores,
355 All with weary task fordone.
Now the wasted brands do glow,
Whilst the screech-owl, screeching loud,
Puts the wretch that lies in woe
In remembrance of a shroud.
360 Now it is the time of night
That the graves, all gaping wide,
Every one lets forth his sprite,
In the church-way paths to glide.
And we fairies, that do run
365 By the triple Hecate's team
From the presence of the sun,
Following darkness like a dream,
Now are frolic. Not a mouse
Shall disturb this hallowed house.
370 I am sent with broom before,
To sweep the dust behind the door.

Enter OBERON *and* TITANIA *with their train.*

OBERON
Through the house give glimmering light
By the dead and drowsy fire,
Every elf and fairy sprite

---

365 *Hecate* "triple" because she was known by three names. She was a goddess of th
moon (and, therefore, abroad at night like the fairies).

since we have stayed up so late tonight.
This obviously crude play has cheated
the sleepy pace of night. Sweet friends, go to bed.
350 For two weeks we'll hold this celebration
in nightly entertainments and new delights.
They exit.
Enter PUCK, *with a broom.*

PUCK
Now the hungry lion roars,
And the wolf howls at the moon,
While the sleeping plowman snores,
355 Exhausted from his weary tasks.
Now the used-up firewood glows,
While the screech owl, screeching loud,
Makes the wretched man who lies in pain
Think of a coffin.
360 Now is the time of night
That graves, all wide open,
Each lets forth a ghost
To glide down the church paths.
And we fairies—who run
365 Beside the three-named Hecate's team
From the presence of the sun,
Following darkness like a dream—
Now we are merry. Not a mouse
Shall disturb this sacred house.
370 I have been sent ahead with a broom
To sweep the dust from behind the door.
Enter OBERON *and* TITANIA *with all their followers.*

OBERON
Through this house, give glimmering light
From the dead and sleepy fire.
Every elf and fairy,

375 Hop as light as bird from brier;
And this ditty, after me,
Sing, and dance it trippingly.

TITANIA
First, rehearse your song by rote,
To each word a warbling note.
380 Hand in hand, with fairy grace,
Will we sing, and bless this place.
[*Song and dance.*]

OBERON
Now, until the break of day,
Through this house each fairy stray.
To the best bride-bed will we,
385 Which by us shall blessed be;
And the issue there create
Ever shall be fortunate.
So shall all the couples three
Ever true in loving be;
390 And the blots of Nature's hand
Shall not in their issue stand;
Never mole, harelip, nor scar,
Nor mark prodigious, such as are
Despised in nativity,
395 Shall upon their children be.
With this field-dew consecrate,
Every fairy take his gait,
And each several chamber bless,
Through this palace, with sweet peace;
400 And the owner of it blest
Ever shall in safety rest.
Trip away; make no stay;
Meet me all by break of day.
[*Exeunt* OBERON, TITANIA, *and train.*]

ROBIN GOODFELLOW
If we shadows have offended,
405 Think but this, and all is mended,
That you have but slumb'red here

375 Hop as lightly as a bird from a twig.
And sing this song after me,
And dance it with spirit.

TITANIA
First, rehearse your song from memory.
To each word, add a musical note.
380 Hand in hand, with fairy grace,
We will sing and bless this place.
(They sing and dance.)

OBERON
Now, until the break of day,
Each fairy must scatter through this house.
We will go to the best bridal bed,
385 Which will be blessed by us.
And the children there conceived
Shall always be fortunate.
Also, all three couples shall
Be forever lovingly faithful.
390 And Nature's occasional deformities
Shall not appear in their children.
Not a mole, harelip, or scar,
Or unnatural birthmark, such as are
Despised in newborn babies,
395 Will be upon their children.
With this consecrated dew from the field,
Every fairy make his way
And bless each and every chamber
Throughout this palace with sweet peace.
400 And the owner of it, once blessed,
Will rest forever in safety.
Skip away; do not stop.
All of you meet me at break of day.
All exit except PUCK.

PUCK
If we shadows have offended you,
405 Just imagine this and all will be mended:
Imagine that you were just sleeping here

While these visions did appear.
And this weak and idle theme,
No more yielding but a dream,
410 Gentles, do not reprehend.
If you pardon, we will mend.
And, as I am an honest Puck,
If we have unearned luck
Now to 'scape the serpent's tongue,
415 We will make amends ere long;
Else the Puck a liar call.
So, good night unto you all.
Give me your hands, if we be friends,
And Robin shall restore amends.
[*Exit.*]

While these visions appeared.
And this weak and silly play
Is no more than a dream.
410 Gentlemen and ladies do not scold us.
If you forgive us, we'll make amends.
And, as I am honest Puck,
If we have the undeserved luck
To escape the hissing of the audience,
415 We'll make it up to you before long.
If we do not, call Puck a liar.
So, good night to you all.
Give me your applause, if we are friends.
And Robin will make amends.
He exits.

THE PLAY IN REVIEW:

A Teacher and Student Supplement

Between Acts: Study Questions

1. **What conflict is introduced in Scene 1?**

   Scene 1 introduces the six mortal lovers and the conflict between them. As the play opens, the first couple—Theseus, duke of Athens, and Hippolyta, queen of the Amazons—are contentedly planning their marriage. This harmony is disrupted when Egeus appears before Theseus to demand a ruling on a domestic problem. Egeus complains that his daughter Hermia refuses to marry Demetrius, the man approved by Egeus. Hermia wishes to marry Lysander instead. Theseus decrees Hermia must obey her father. Her only alternatives are death or banishment to a nunnery.

   Theseus' ruling also creates conflict for Helena. She is still in love with Demetrius, though he abandoned her for her friend Helena.

2. **How does Shakespeare suddenly shift the center of attention in the first scene?**

   Because the play opens with details of the courtship of Theseus and Hippolyta, the reader might expect the entire play to concern these royal lovers. Instead, Shakespeare shifts the reader's attention to the love story of more common men and women. Shakespeare typically spotlights more lowly men and women in his comedies in contrast to his tragedies, where the heroes and heroines are of high station.

3. **What arguments does Lysander use to claim his right to court Hermia?**

   Lysander says he is equal to Demetrius in wealth and status. He further notes that Demetrius is an inconstant lover since he wooed and then abandonded Helena.

4. **What are the differences between Hermia and Helena?**

Hermia is spirited and determined. She refuses to accept either the orders of her father or her ruler. Only when Hermia is with Lysander is she docile. In contrast, Helena is much more submissive and passive. While Hermia plots her moves with determination and forcefulness, Helena acts almost against her will and out of desperation.

5. **What do Hermia's resistance, Lysander's scheme, and Helena's betrayal of her friends suggest about loyalties?**

Love is the supreme value to all three characters; no loyalty is higher than devotion to a lover. Hermia refuses to bow to her father or her state ruler. In the matters of the heart, she retains "sovereignty." Lysander, too, boldly disregards his sovereign's decree and proposes they escape "sharp Athenian law" by eloping. Helena, when she reveals Hermia and Lysander's confidential plans to Demetrius, also proves that love is a stronger bond than friendship. Even after Hermia's kind farewell-wishes for her "sweet playfellow" and Helena's own admission that Demetrius is unworthy, Helena betrays her best friend in the name of love.

6. **What are Helena's views on love? How does this compare to the view of love offered throughout the play?**

Helena says love is blind, lacking in judgment and reason, as well as being inconstant. She compares herself to Hermia and remarks, "Through Athens I am thought as fair as she." However, she recognizes that this valuation means nothing because Demetrius does not think so. He continues in his blind error of worshiping the indifferent Hermia (ironically, Helena specially states Demetrius dotes on "Hermia's eyes"). And Helena frankly admits she mistakenly continues to worship Demetrius.

Being ensnared by illogical affection is, in Hermia's opinion, just the nature of love. Her opinion of love is vividly captured in her reference to Cupid, the blindfolded child-god of love, who capriciously shoots his magic arrows and engenders love. This view fits the play's theme of love as a form of lunacy which abruptly seizes a person for no rational reason.

7. **How does the inclusion of the craftsmen shift the atmosphere and tone of the play?**

In the beginning of Act I, the audience was immersed in the classical world of Athens. But with the introduction of Quince, Bottom, and their companions, the scene suddenly moves to a very Elizabethan world. Here the characters have names common to Shakespeare's day. And not only are their names common—these workingmen sharply contrast with the nobles and more cultured characters of Scene 1. Shakespeare clearly delineates this difference between the two groups with the use of speech. While the lovers and fairies generally speak in poetry, the craftsmen talk in prose. Their speech is also dotted with crudities and more contemporary references than the other characters.

The inclusion of the craftsmen also introduces a broader, more burlesque tone to the comedy, as well as satire. Enchanted or not, these mortals are always fools, laughable in their ignorant pretensions. Yet in their very attempts to emulate their betters, the craftsmen often unknowingly satirize the behavior of the nobles and lovers.

8. **What is the significance of the play that Bottom and his friends are rehearsing as Scene 2 opens?**

The play-within-the-play is based on the myth of Pyramus and Thisby, two Babylonian youths. Pyramus and Thisby fall in love and want to marry, but their parents forbid the match. The play serves as a parallel to Hermia and Lysander's story. Like Pyramus and Thisby, Hermia and Lysander are forbidden to marry by a parent. Also, Hermia and Lysander flee to the woods, just as Pyramus and Thisby do.

However, as events unfold, the tragedy of Pyramus and Thisby will evolve from a parallel to an ironic contrast with the mortal lovers' story and the play-within-a-play.

9. Why will May Day bring the climax of the play?

Four important events are scheduled to occur on May Day. First, Theseus and Hippolyta plan to be married on that day. Second, Hermia must give her decision about marrying Demetrius on the first of May. Third, the craftsmen plan their drama for that day to celebrate the duke's wedding. Fourth, May Day is a special, magic time for the fairies. Thus on all four levels of the plot, climactic events are scheduled to occur.

May Day is also symbolically significant. That holiday evoked certain images for Elizabethans, as did the different holiday at summer solstice—Midsummer Day. Shakespeare probably combined the two dates because both holidays were associated with love, fertility, and a harmless delirium or madness. In a play filled with lovers' quarrels, magic, and wild waking dreams, there can be no more appropriate symbolic climax.

10. Describe Bottom the Weaver.

Bottom is a wonderfully comic character. He is a natural ham, eagerly volunteering to take every role in the play and certain that he can perform them admirably. He also continually prompts Quince, the troupe's director, and offers ridiculous directorial suggestions. Bottom's eagerness far outstrips his learning. He bungles names and mixes up words. However, his bravado seems to impress his friends, who like and respect him.

11. What are some of the unpleasant aspects of love revealed in Act I?

Shakespeare shows that love can be tyrannical. For example, while Egeus loves his daughter, he forces her to make a terrible choice. If Hermia does not bow to his wishes, she faces either death or a vow of lifelong chastity.

Helena's sufferings also prove that love can be unkind and fickle. Her unrequited love for Demetrius makes her miserable and strips her of pride. She demonstrates, too, that all love is not equal. She willingly betrays her good friend Hermia just to be able to talk to Demetrius.

12. What are some of the magical elements in Act II, Scene 1?

You need go no further than the title of *A Midsummer Night's Dream* to find magic. As previously discussed (question 9), Elizabethans viewed Midsummer's Day and May Day as a period of madness when fairies were everywhere and magic was powerful. Some of these fairies are actually featured in the play, too. Oberon and Titania, the king and queen of the fairies, are introduced. Puck, Oberon's servant, also appears to work his mischievous magic everywhere. The magical mood is sustained by the setting of moonlight and the mysterious wood.

13. How does Puck suit the mood and plot of the play?

Puck is known for his delight in deception, particularly his practical jokes against the more common mortals. The transformation of Bottom is a classic example of Puck's taste in magic. This brand of light-hearted mischief suits a comedy where magical confusions abound but no one is seriously hurt. The other side to Puck's personality is in character with the happy ending, too. When Puck is called by his proper name, he helps mortals: "You do their work, and they shall have good luck."

In a purely mechanical sense, Puck is also essential to the plot development. As Oberon's messenger, he carries out and more importantly miscarries the fairy king's orders. It is Puck's mistakes that produce the farcical mix-up among the mortal lovers. His role is that of an impish Cupid who haphazardly sparks love.

14. What conflict exists between Oberon and Titania? What is the tone of their disagreement?

Puck reveals that Oberon is furious with Titania. Oberon wants Titania to give him an Indian boy she has in her care. Titania refuses because the boy's mother, now dead, was once her beloved attendant. The quarrel seems a petty disagreement, and the jealousy of the fairies adds to this impression. Titania accuses her spouse of loving Hippolyta, Theseus' bride. Oberon, in turn, accuses Titania of loving Theseus and of influencing him to abandon several lovers. The notion is ridiculous, considering the size difference between the mortals and the tiny fairies.

But the contest of wills between the fairy king and queen has more serious effects. The displeased Oberon has caused storms, floods, rotting crops, and rheumatic diseases to occur throughout the world. Oberon says that when he has the Indian boy, this destruction will cease.

15. What is Oberon's plan for forcing Titania to agree to his demand?

Oberon remembers that he once saw Cupid shoot a love arrow at a beautiful virgin. The arrow missed the girl and struck a white pansy, turning the flower purple with desire. Oberon tells Puck to take the juice from that pansy and drop it onto Titania's eyelids. The juice will cause Titania to fall in love with the first living creature she sees. Oberon believes that he will be able to persuade or force Titania to give up the boy while she is in this state of foolish infatuation.

16. What is ironic or symbolic about Oberon's magic potion and the view of love as presented in the play?

The magic potion comes from an arrow shot by Cupid. This potion of the god of love's, who is often depicted as shooting his arrows while blindfolded, produces blind love. This symbolism carries over into the manner in which the juice is applied—directly in the victim's eyes, blinding that person literally and figuratively.

The theme of love being bred through the lover's eyes is expanded when love is also seen as being bred by the beloved's eyes. For example, Helena complains Demetrius "errs, doting on Hermia's eyes" and envies Hermia's "blessed and attractive eyes." Lysander, blinded by the magic potion, declares that "Reason becomes the marshal to my will / And leads me to your eyes; where I o'erlook / Love's stories, written in Love's richest book." Similarly, the bewitched Demetrius is immediately struck by Helena's eyes. "To what my love, shall I compare thine eyne?" he exclaims.

The love produced by Oberon's potion stands for any love which is sparked by romance and not reason. That kind of love may flourish in the wood but is doomed in the city. When Hermia wishes that her father could see things through her eyes, affected by love, she is reproved by Theseus. "Rather your eyes must with his judgment look" he states.

17. What does Oberon's decision to use the magic potion on Titania indicate about his character? How does this compare or contrast to his motivation in using the potion on the human lovers?

Oberon's scheme to anoint Titania's eyes shows his determination to have his way. Oberon's plan also indicates that he loves intrigue and enjoys a joke at another's expense. This same desire to have things the way he deems proper and to meddle in others' lives is also seen in his interest in the mortal lovers. But a softer side of the fairy king's personality is revealed as well. He pities Helena when he hears her cruelly spurned by

Demetrius. As king, Oberon may wish to punish the scornful Demetrius, but as a lover, his heart is touched by the loyal Helena.

18. **What causes Puck to think that Lysander is the Athenian youth whose eyes he is to anoint?**

Lysander and Hermia become lost in the woods and decide to settle down there for the night. Lysander insists that it is perfectly proper for them to sleep side by side. But Hermia objects, saying that for virtue's sake, her lover must sleep farther off. When Puck chances across the pair, he believes he has found the Athenian couple Oberon told him about. He thinks Lysander is sleeping so far apart from Hermia because he disdains her. Therefore, like the blindfolded love god Cupid, Puck blindly and mistakenly works his magic and anoints Lysander's eyes.

19. **What is ironic about Lysander's declaration of love for Helena?**

Lysander, affected by the magic love potion, falls in love with Helena (who, happening to walk by, has awakened Lysander). When Helena confusedly protests that Lysander loves Hermia, he denies this. He insists instead that his change of heart is a voluntary, sensible decision. "The will of man is by his reason swayed; / And reason says you are the worthier maid," he explains.

Lysander's argument would have struck an audience of Shakepeare's day as ironic in another respect. Elizabethans never equated reason with love. In fact, Lysander's reasonable justification of his love would merely prove him a love-struck lunatic.

Lysander's language is ironic, too. He has been emotionally blinded by the flower juice dropped (appropriately enough) in his eyes. However, he claims his love is sparked when he can "see" Helena's heart and "o'erlook Love's stories" in her eyes.

20. **How does Lysander react toward Hermia after the juice is placed in his eyes?**

Under the spell of the nectar, Lysander compares Hermia to an overly sweet thing of which he has eaten too much or a heresy that he regrets. He hopes he will never see Hermia again. He leaves her—alone, defenseless, and still asleep—while he pursues Helena.

21. **What is the mood as Act III, Scene 1 opens?**

The mood is comic and lighthearted, highlighting the buffoonishness of Bottom and his fellow actors. As the scene opens, the troupe is in the glade where Titania is sleeping, rehearsing their play. They take their production very seriously and believe that their convincing dramatics will be impressive and perhaps frightening. They worry, for example, that the ladies in the audience will be distressed when Bottom as Pyramus draws a sword and kills himself. They also fear that Snout's portrayal of the lion will terrify the ladies and therefore displease the duke. The troupe decides that two speeches are necessary to reassure the audience. This concern is amusing considering the actors' real ineptness at acting.

22. **Why is Bottom's transformation ironic?**

Puck's mischievous transformation of Bottom is ironic and symbolic. One irony is the moment the fairy chooses to cast his spell. Just as Bottom rehearses his line, "If I were fair, Thisby, I were only thine," Puck magically changes Bottom's head into an ass' head. The ironies increase when Titania, influenced by the love charm, awakens and beholds her "angel." Her praise of the ridiculous weaver shows how foolish love can be.

Of course, the fact that Bottom is given an ass' head is the source of many puns. In the Elizabethan days, as in modern times, ass' meant "fool." The fact that Bottom wears an ass's head—read either "fool's head" or "the head of an animal"—again emphasizes that love and reason do not mix.

A further irony of Bottom's transformation is the contrast he makes with Titania's other changeling. Bottom is a changeling in two senses: he has been stolen away by the fairies, and he has been changed by their magic. And just as Titania dotes on the little Indian boy who has become her changeling, so she adores Bottom. The obvious irony comes in the comparison between the appearance of the two changelings. The description of the Indian boy paints him as lovely and charming. The clownish Bottom, on the other hand, is so hideous in his ass's head that he scares even his friends away. However, the charmed Titania thinks he is beautiful and willingly gives up her other changeling to Oberon while infatuated with Bottom.

3. What does Bottom's reaction to Titania's protestations of love say about his character?

Bottom's reaction shows him to be a rustic philosopher and further develops his character as the self-confident, comic clown who loves to play a role. When Titania first swears her love, he objects with uncharacteristic humbleness, saying she has little reason for that. Then he philosophizes, "And yet, to say the truth, reason and love keep little company nowadays." Lowly, ridiculous character that he is, Bottom is here given the wisdom to express a major theme of *A Midsummer Night's Dream*.

Despite his objection, Bottom is easily persuaded by Titania's flattery and the regalness of his position. He enjoys playing the lord, though he carries the role off with as many comic gaffes as he will later play Pyramus.

4. Why are Titania's declarations of love for Bottom so amusing?

Titania's love speeches are couched in poetry and exquisitely expressed. Bottom, the recipient of these tributes, is a grotesque contrast to the images Titania's words evoke. This contrast makes Titania's words wonderfully ironic—as when she she tries to compliment her lover by saying "Thou art as wise as thou art beautiful." The final twist to the love scene is that Titania, blindly enamored though she is, still cannot tolerate Bottom's loquacity. She tells her attendants, "Tie up my love's tongue, bring him silently."

25. What theme is developed by Hermia's "snake dream"?

Immediately after the enchanted Lysander deserts Hermia, she awakens calling for him. She has dreamt that "a serpent eat my heart away, / And you sat smiling at his cruel prey." This dream symbolizes what has actually happened. Hermia's heart—her love for Lysander—has been inadvertently destroyed by Helena and Puck. And in his drugged state, Lysander now scorns Hermia.

Hermia's dream shows the complex relation between dreams and reality in the play. In the fairy world of the woods, dreams and reality merge. In this twilight world, the characters confront the terrible conflicts of reality, yet suffer no real harm. As Hermia's heart is still whole after her snake dream, so Lysander and Hermia will be reconciled when they awaken from their midsummer night's dream.

26. How do Puck and Oberon react when they learn Puck has mistaken the identities of the mortal lovers?

Oberon is distressed by the mix-up and orders Puck to hurriedly amend things. The fairy king's description of Helena once again reveals his pity and concern for her. There may be a bit of envy in Oberon's displeasure, too. One suspects that he also does not relish this joke, unlike Titania's foolish infatuation, because he did not plan it. In any case, Oberon is not even mildly amused by the confusion and scolds Puck, suspecting his servant of deliberate mischief-making. "This is thy negligence. Still thou mistak'st, / Or else committ'st thy knaveries willfully," he accuses.

Puck, on the other hand, is enormously entertained by the comedy of errors. He treats the confrontations between the lovers as a farcical drama which can afford him amusement. The "pageant" in fact merely confirms his view of humans. "Lord, what fools these mortals be!" he exclaims, expressing the observation that the real, offstage audience also is forced to draw. The lovers' behavior also matches his philosophical notions about the constancy of love. He says to Oberon, "Fate o'er-rules, that, one man holding troth, / A million fail, confounding oath on oath." With this statement, Puck seems to excuse his mistake by pleading that he is just an agent of inexplicable fate.

27. What makes the scene where all the lovers confront one another comic instead of tragic?

First, the scene is comic because we know the effects of the love potion can be reversed. Oberon confided this information to the audience earlier when he schemed to humiliate Titania.

Second, the scene is comic because it is a complete reversal from the earlier situation. Now Lysander and Demetrius are eager to pursue a girl neither one cared for just an hour ago, while ignoring and insulting the maiden they both had desired.

Third, the reactions of the characters themselves make us laugh at them rather than weep. Helena assumes that Lysander's and Demetrius' declarations are mockery. Her attitude prevents tragedy from occurring. If she took Lysander's vows seriously and felt flattered instead, the shock of awakening from her midsummer night's dream would be brutal.

Hermia's reaction also plays on the comedy of the scene. The fiery Hermia does not take the tragic route and kill herself like Thisby when she believes she has lost her lover. Instead, she is ready to take offense at Helena's words and physically fight her. Helena meanwhile comically pleads for protection from Hermia, while unintentionally delivering more insults to the pugnacious Hermia.

Lysander and Demetrius add to the comedy, trying

to outdo the other in swearing their love to Helena. Their proposed duel is also amusing because their bloody threats prove hollow in the end when they are diverted by Puck.

Fourth, Puck's reaction gives the audience its cue. When Oberon scolds him, Puck innocently swears that the confusion was all a mistake—although a humorous mistake. He says, "And so far am I glad it so did sort, / As this their jangling I esteem a sport."

28. How are all the confusions among the human lovers resolved?

Puck separates Demetrius and Lysander by taunting each in the imitated voice of his opponent. Then he puts all the lovers to sleep, close to one another. Finally, he removes the spell from Lysander's eyes but leaves Demetrius enchanted. Now the couples will be happily paired when they awaken.

29. What does the resolution of Titania's quarrel with Oberon imply about the fairy dreams?

While in her enchanted dream state, Titania willingly gives Oberon the fairy child. This action, which resolves the quarrel between the fairy king and queen, shows that the magical dreams can bring people to their senses. When the spell is removed and Titania is awakened, she contentedly reunites with her husband.

30. How are the green world and the city world reconciled?

The green world of the fairies and the city world of the Athenians are reconciled when Theseus comes to the woods to hunt. As could be expected, Theseus brings his city world with him—his bride-to-be, his courtiers, and his trained hounds. Yet Theseus' remarks clue the audience that the mood is right for a reconciliation between the two worlds. The duke remarks that he has come to the wood to hear the harmonious cries of his hounds join in "musical confusion" with the echoes of the mountains. Hippolyta too relishes this "musical discord" and "sweet thunder." The symbol of the hunting dogs shows that the two worlds of city and wood can mix together in pleasing, if weirdly inharmonious, music.

This symbolic foreshadowing is fulfilled on the level of plot. The duke finds the sleeping lovers, who awaken at his approach—this time paired as Oberon intended. Undoubtedly affected by such influences of the green world as the May Day atmosphere and his own romantic mood as he prepares for his wedding, the officious ruler bends. Theseus overrules Egeus' objections and puts the blessings of the state on this match made by fairies. In fact, he not only grants the couples permission to marry, but also invites them to be wed in the same ceremony that will unite him to Hippolyta.

The fairies make their peace with the city world, too. With the quarrel patched up between Oberon and Titania, they forget their jealousy of Theseus and Hippolyta. Indeed, the fairies grow as generous as their human counterparts. Oberon proposes that he and Titania "dance in Duke Theseus' house triumphantly / And bless it to all fair prosperity."

The forces as well as the personalities of the green world and the city world are reconciled. The dreams and magic of the green world fade to the waking reality of Athens. However the effects of the wood—the hazy memories, sense of wonder, and most importantly, the love bonds sealed between the characters—remain with the mortals as they return to the city.

31. What obvious differences are there in the play between night and day?

Night is the time the moon reigns and brings lunacy. It also is the time for dreams and enchantment, when the fairies are most active and work their magic on sleeping mortals (and Titania). The delusions that make up the action of the play begin and climax at night. In contrast, day is the time of normalcy, when reason rules and dreams are put away. Night is the setting for the green world, and day belongs to the city.

32. What is the state of the young Athenian couples and Bottom when they awaken from their trances?

Both the lovers and Bottom awaken confused. They wonder if the events they remember really happened or if the occurrences were just the imaginings of a dream. The dreams also seem vague. "These things seem small and undistinguishable, / Like far-off mountains turned into clouds," says Demetrius. Bottom expresses the same sentiment with his typical comic clumsiness, "I have had a dream, past the wit of man to say what dream it was. Man is but an ass if he go about to expound this dream." Then ass that he was and is, Bottom precedes to do just that with hopeless results.

Yet the effects of the midsummer dreams do not completely disappear. After Theseus awakens the lovers, they wonder if they are still dreaming. Like Shakespeare's play itself, the dreams remain with Bottom and the lovers to amaze and, in Demetrius' case at least, to influence.

33. How has Bottom's absence affected his friends?

Bottom's friends are very upset by his absence and have begun to extol the virtues of the weaver. They praise the wit and sweet voice of Bottom (the man who has just lately been saddled with an ass' head). Without Bottom, the craftsmen must scrap their dreams of a sixpence a day for life as a reward for their great play. As Quince says, "You have not a man in all Athens able to discharge Pyramus but he." But in the nick of time, Bottom reappears in a bustle to herd the actors to the palace.

34. What parallels does Theseus draw between the lover, the madman, and the poet?

Theseus says all three types of people are ruled by

riotous imaginations. The madman imagines all manner of devils, the lover sees beauty where it does not exist, and the poet gives airy thoughts form and solidity. Theseus, who is after all the arguing voice for reason in the play, implies these kinds of people are pitiable. But as the previous acts of the play have demonstrated, the force of imagination cannot be denied or belittled. Even greater testament to the beauty and strength of imagination is *A Midsummer Night's Dream* itself. From the audience's point of view, Theseus is just an imaginative (re)creation who will endure as long as Shakespeare's play does.

35. What are Theseus' expectations about the craftsmen's play? Why are those expectations in some measure ironic?

Theseus expects a whimsical piece, which he will certainly find in a play titled: "A tedious brief scene of young Pyramus / And his love Thisby; very tragical mirth." He decides to hear the play, swearing to Hippolyta (who fears that the players will be mocked) that he will be understanding of the players' limitations. He protests that he values most the kind of love and humble honor which speak the least.

But if Theseus expects "tongue-tied simplicity" and limited speeches, he is bound to be surprised by Bottom. Even the infatuated Titania complained about Bottom's garrulousness. And after his dramatic death speech, Bottom is ready to return to the stage for the epilogue.

Moreover, Theseus compares the craftsmen's offering to the speeches foreigners tried to offer him. These foreigners were so flustered and impressed by Theseus' reputation that they could not stammer out their welcomes. The craftsmen, too, intend their offering as an honor to the duke. However, the farcical turn their enactment gives to the Pyramus and Thisby story satirizes all the lovers in the play.

36. **How does *A Midsummer Night's Dream* resemble a masque? What function does the play-within-a-play serve in the masque?**

A Midsummer Night's Dream is often compared to a masque, a court drama filled with music and dances. Masques were extremely stylized works, with carefully balanced structures and elaborate poetic speeches. A masque often featured allegorical characters and sometimes supernatural beings, too.

Given this definition, the body of *A Midsummer Night's Dream* can be seen as a masque. The drama is heavily supplemented with songs, poetic chants, and celebratory dances. The plot as well as the language is heavily stylized. The four stages of action—the nobility, the mortal lovers, the fairies, and the craftsmen—carefully interact, and all four levels of the plot climax in the same scene. The fairies; magical wood; and mystical, moonlit, May Day spirit give the drama its supernatural tone.

An antimasque often accompanied a masque. This piece was a farce or a realistic comedy which sometimes commented on the masque. The Pyramus and Thisby play is like an antimasque in that it burlesques a traditional love story that parallels Hermia and Lysander's situation. Bottom and his friends also resemble the characters in the antimasque, who were frequently rustics.

37. **How does the play-within-a-play serve as a parody of dramatic traditions?**

The craftsmen's enactment of the Pyramus and Thisby myth is a parody of the Senecan tradition of tragedy in Elizabethan drama. The Senecan formula was typified by long-winded speeches and commentaries, intense expressions of sorrow and other emotions, and liberal use of rhetorical devices. Shakespeare pokes fun at this tradition by grossly exaggerating these devices in the rustics' play.

The play-within-a-play and *A Midsummer Night's Dream* as a whole also ridicule the Senecan philosophical tradition. One of the tenets of Seneca's stoic philosophy was that tragedy resulted when passion overcame reason. The craftsmen's play mocks this premise by so wildly exaggerating the tragedy that it becomes farce. *A Midsummer Night's Dream* as a whole also shows that comedy—not tragedy—and delicious, if foolish, love result from passion.

Besides parodying the Senecan tragedies, the craftsmen's play makes fun of certain tendencies in many Elizabethan dramas. The makeshift props, outrageously poor and ignorant acting, and overly long and explicit prologues of their play were all typical, annoying aspects of Elizabethan theater.

38. What purpose is served by Puck's epilogue?

Puck's epilogue is a traditional device. Usually such epilogues apologized for the play—as Puck's does. But Puck's epilogue is more than an exercise in custom; it also completes the play in a number of ways.

First, Puck's epilogue ties up a loose end. Theseus prevented Bottom, the clown of the mortal world, from delivering the epilogue to the Pyramus and Thisby drama. Now the clown of the fairy world, Puck, steps forward to deliver an apology that could well suit both the internal drama and the play as a whole.

The epilogue resolves the final conflicts in the play, too. Blessings have been given at each level—the actors have been blessed by Theseus, the actors have "blessed" all the marriages with their play, Theseus has blessed the other two couples, the young Athenians have blessed the duke's marriage, and the fairies have blessed the mortals. Now a blessing is extended at the final level. The impish Puck shows his kind side and promises to "restore amends" to his good friends in the offstage audience.

The epilogue also serves to remind us of an important motif in the play—the dream. Like the drugged lovers who believe the confusion in the woods was a dream, we are invited to believe "That you have but slumb'red here / While these visions did appear."

Finally, the epilogue harkens back to the theme raised in Theseus' speech at the beginning of this act. There the duke stated that love, delusions, and poetry all have their root in the dreams of imagination. Given this connection, *A Midsummer Night's Dream* can be seen as self-reflexive—a work *about* the power of imagination that, through marvelous poetry and engaging action, *demonstrates* the power of imagination.

The Play's the Thing: Discussion Questions

Motivation:

1. **What part does magic play in *A Midsummer Night's Dream*?**

Magic plays a large role in the play. Most of the conflicts of the play arise when the city world of reason meets the fairy world of magic. When fairies squeeze the magic juice of a flower, touched by Cupid's arrow, upon the eyes of Demetrius, Lysander, and Titania, the major events of the play are set in motion. Bottom's transformation adds to the magical confusion and comedy. Eventually these four transformations affect the lives of every character in the play.

Magic infects the atmosphere as well as the plot of the play. May Day and Midsummer Day were occasions for special magic, associated with love and fertility. Lovers were spurred by the atmosphere to wild displays of their affection.

Magic is also a metaphor for love in the play. Magic, like romantic love, leads the characters to foolish, blind action. Despite the wild effects that magic and love can produce, no harm arises from either spell. In fact, the effect of both forces in *A Midsummer Night's Dream* is comic. When the magic fades, or the insane intensity of passion passes, only a confused, dreamlike remembrance remains.

2. **In some of Shakespeare's plays, fate is the unseen motivator of mortals. Which character acts as fate or the motivator in *A Midsummer Night's Dream*?**

Oberon, king of the fairies, is one major motivator. It is Oberon who bewitches his own wife and sorts out the lovers into neat and contented pairs. Like Prospero in *The Tempest,* Oberon is a benevolent force who enjoys his power but sympathizes with those over whom he wields it. However, Oberon is not completely in control. But even Puck's mistakes in carrying out Oberon's orders are in keeping with the Elizabethans' characterization of fate. Puck's mistakes bring inexplicable, abrupt, and apparently cruel changes, even as fate was seen to do.

3. **Of what significance is Puck's error in administering the magic potion?**

Around that error revolves a large part of the action and comedy of the play. When the magic goes awry, the situation among the lovers is completely reversed. Conflict arises from every encounter among the young Athenian couples. Helena rejects both Lysander and Demetrius because she believes the men are mocking her. The drugged men are spurned by their new love, Helena, and at each others' throats contesting their affection. Hermia is distressed by Lysander's sudden change of heart and furious with Helena for stealing him away. The climax of the play occurs when Oberon steps in and restores order to the tangled relationships.

4. **Love in all its guises is the subject of *A Midsummer Night's Dream.* Trace the development of one of the symbols or metaphors for love in the play.**

Responses will vary. Students may discuss how love is depicted as a dove, serpent, blindness, madness, mystery, union, enchantment, moonlight, dream, curse, blessing, peace, and war.

5. **Give an example from the play of a force that opposes love.**

Responses will vary (particularly depending on student's response to question 4). Students may discuss how reason, law, authority, hate, daylight, war, fate, and jealousy work against love.

6. **Why is Oberon's magical henchman referred to by two names, Puck and Robin Goodfellow?**

Traditionally a Puck is a roguish imp, at times even an instrument of the devil. Robin Goodfellow, on the other hand, is a symbol of the good and gentle English supernatural spirit who supposedly haunted the forest of Arden. Shakespeare combines the character of both figures in Puck. His Puck delights in making mischief and proving "what fools these mortals be," but the fairy also aids those who address him politely.

7. **What is the significance of day and night in *A Midsummer Night's Dream*?**

Order and rationality, as symbolized by Theseus and his Athenian court, rule during the daylight hours. But at night, the magic of the fairy world is particularly potent. At that time, the fears of humans are most active—Bottom's transformation seems all the more terrifying for occurring at night. Nor is horror the only occupation of the mind at night; romantic imagination is also at a peak. Especially in the moonlight, love can become a wild, lunatic love. Even sleep is unsafe, for the dreams and nightmares that occur often seem as real as reality. In fact, those dreams are reality in *A Midsummer Night's Dream*.

8. **What is a possible message of the play-within-a-play?**

The message depends on whether one takes the Pyramus and Thisby drama at face value or accepts a satirical view. At face value, the message seems to be that "the course of true love never did run smooth," as Lysander remarks. Pyramus and Thisby are separated from one another by their parents' disapproval. When they resort to meeting in the woods, tragedy results. A lion frightens Thisby. Pyramus, finding her bloody cloak, believes she is dead and kills himself out of grief. Thisby discovers her dead lover and also commits suicide. This tragic ending seems to imply a second message: blind passion can lead to tragedy.

However, if the play-within-a-play is seen as a satire, these messages take a comic turn. The view that the play-within-the-play is a satire is more in tune with the craftsmen's enactment of the myth, as well as the rest of *A Midsummer Night's Dream.* While Hermia and Lysander, Helena and Demetrius, Oberon and Titania, and even Theseus and Hippolyta have rocky moments in their relationships, tragedy does not result from their misunderstandings. Though their love is blind, lunatic, and intense at points, passion does not destroy them. The play-within-the-play—as ridiculously performed by the rustics—serves merely as a mirror of the lovers' silliness and exaggerated emotions.

Philosophy:

1. **What is the relationship between the microcosm and macrocosm in the play?**

The two worlds seem closely affected by each other. Oberon and Titania's quarrel disrupts the microcosm, splitting the fairy world in two. This argument affects the macrocosm, or the world at large. Society as a whole is touched when mortals stumble into the midst of the argument and have their love lives turned upside down. In fact, the midsummer madness Oberon unleashes to force Titania to give up the Indian boy turns reason upside down. Finally, the macrocosm of the natural world is affected by the fairies' fight. Oberon has bred storms, floods, diseases, and confused the seasons to irritate Titania.

The macrocosm also affects the microcosm. The May Day/Midsummer Day atmosphere of fertility, lunatic love, and magic influences all the characters. Nature has its influence, too. The heady flowers (including the magical pansy, or love-in-idleness), romantic moonlight, and mysterious wood spark and sustain the characters' dreamy, romantic obsessions.

2. **What is the mythic significance of the sun and moon? How do those symbols compare with the forces of reason and magic in *A Midsummer Night's Dream*?**

The god Apollo (also known as Phoebus) was the classical mythic figure associated with the sun. Apollo was viewed as the personification of wisdom, learning, and reason. His character clearly suits the spirit of the city world where orderly reason and sanity rule.

The multiple personifications of the moon in classical myths makes this symbol more complex. One important characterization of the moon was the goddess Artemis (Diana). She was viewed as a superb huntress, as well as the embodiment of chastity. In this manifestation, the moon seems more in tune with Theseus' world. Theseus is a devotee of hunting. And enforced chastity is one of the cruel punishments with which he threatens Hermia. "To live a barren sister all your life, / Chanting faint hymns to the cold fruitless moon."

However, in other personifications, the moon is connected with wilder, more fertile forces. Hecate, a moon goddess, was associated with mystery and magic. As Lucina, the goddess assisting in childbirth, the moon is connected with fertility. Both of these traits are clearly associated with the fairy world.

Even as the city world and the green world are reconciled in the play, so the symbols of sun and moon are linked. Apollo and Artemis were twins.

3. **Give two other examples of classical myths that are mentioned in the play and explain their significance.**

Responses will vary. Students may mention the myth of Pyramus and Thisby, which parodies and parallels the various threads of the plots. Theseus and Hippolyta are legendary characters, too, and their inclusion in the play provides a framework for the rest of the action (Theseus' decree provokes the escape to the wood, his wedding celebration is the excuse for the rustics' play), furthers themes (rational love, order, love as war), and establishes setting (the noble world of ancient Greece). Cupid, the god of love, prominently figures in the play. His brand of blind, sudden passion captures the essence of love that the bewitched characters experience. There also is mention of Dido, Ariadne, and Aegles, all deserted lovers like Hermia and Helena. References to mythical lovers pursued and never won (Apollo and Daphne) mirror the plight of Helena chasing Demetrius and the two men who pursue her in vain for a time. Finally, throughout the play, nature is vividly personified with references to gods and goddesses. This latter device helps recreate the atmosphere of ancient Greece and breathes a spirit of magic into all aspects of the natural world.

4. **What makes Bottom appealing?**

Even as the pretentious fool, Bottom charms the audience. He plays his roles of great actor, director, noble lover, and even ass with such gusto and self-satisfaction that an audience laughs at rather than pities him. Part of this laughter is directed at ourselves as we acknowledge Puck's statement: "What fools these mortals be!" Other failings of Bottom's character, including his tendency to muddle names and words, contradict himself, and build castles in the air, are just as human and comic.

In addition, Bottom is appealing because he possesses the virtues of many of Shakespeare's other clowns. His admirable points include native common sense, almost accidental wit, an ability to land on his feet, and energetic imagination. This capacity broadens Bottom's role from mere entertainer to commentator.

5. **How is the idea of the watcher and the watched developed in the play?**

In *A Midsummer Night's Dream,* as in dramas such as *Hamlet* and *Macbeth,* Shakespeare develops the idea of the watcher and the watched. Just as the plot of the play is multilayered, so there are many levels upon which the idea of watcher and watched works. The primary watchers are Oberon, who is nearly omniscient, and Puck. Oberon directs the action, Puck tries to carry out his orders, and they both watch in invisible concealment as developments unfold. They observe the delusions of the oblivious Bottom, Titania, and the young Athenian lovers. In turn the Athenians watch each other as they seek to avoid a deserted lover, find a lost beloved, or corner a rival.

Theseus also is a watcher, though not as farsighted as Oberon. His role is to watch and guard order in the city. In addition, he watches the sleeping lovers in the wood and watches over them at the wedding.

The final scene shows three levels of watchers. First, Theseus and his court watch the play put on by the craftsmen. But the nobles and the lovers are being watched in turn by the fairies. Finally, Puck's epilogue makes us aware of the most omniscient watcher of all—the offstage audience.

6. **With what two traditional folk festivals is *A Midsummer Night's Dream* connected?**

The play is connected with both May Day and Midsummer Day, or the summer solstice. Together, these two festive days create visions of holiday happiness, abandon—particularly in love—magic, and the supernatural. The days also were connected with marriage and fertility.

7. **Shakespeare is ever aware of the dichotomy between reality and illusion. Give one example of how this dichotomy is developed through the plot or symbols in the play.**

Responses will vary. Suggested responses include a discussion of the dichotomy between sleeping and waking, dreaming and reality, moonlight and daylight, magic and reason. Other suggestions: the rustics' concern that their audience won't distinguish between nature and art; the delusions of romantic love; the illusion of tragedy and the reality of comedy. Students also might note the theme of the watcher/watched gives the impression the whole play is illusion, mere "pageantry" for the viewer's entertainment.

Encore: Vocabulary Words

The main words in the groups below are taken from *A Midsummer Night's Dream*. Choose the word that is *not* a synonym of the main word.

1. wanes
   a. paints
   b. fades
   c. weakens

2. vexation
   a. annoyance
   b. invention
   c. irritation

3. abjure
   a. forsake
   b. renounce
   c. pretend

4. avouch
   a. lie
   b. declare
   c. assert

5. idolatry
   a. worship
   b. adoration
   c. majesty

6. inconstant
   a. careworn
   b. faithless
   c. fickle

7. edict
   a. law
   b. scroll
   c. order

8. vile
   a. disgusting
   b. ridiculous
   c. foul

9. waggish
   a. sinful
   b. mischievous
   c. playful

10. entreat
   a. beg
   b. plead
   c. rebel

11. knavish
   a. proud
   b. mischievous
   c. devilish

12. beguile
   a. deceive
   b. mislead
   c. surprise

13. progeny
   a. children
   b. lovers
   c. offspring

14. dissension
   a. disagreement
   b. conflict
   c. freedom

15. dote
   a. adore
   b. envy
   c. love

16. disdainful
   a. scornful
   b. lonely
   c. haughty

17. sentinel
   a. boss
   b. guard
   c. watchman

18. languish
   a. return
   b. pine
   c. long

19. dissembling
   a. disguising
   b. changing
   c. masking

20. tedious
   a. tiresome
   b. boring
   c. cheap

21. odious
   a. scented
   b. foul
   c. horrid

22. enamored
   a. educated
   b. charmed
   c. entranced

23. purge
   a. remove
   b. cleanse
   c. decorate

24. lamenting
   a. weeping
   b. grieving
   c. seeking

25. consecrated
   a. blessed
   b. sacred
   c. enormous

26. sojourned
   a. played
   b. visited
   c. lingered

27. disparage
   a. condemn
   b. criticize
   c. watch

28. confederacy
   a. county
   b. league
   c. union

29. loathed
   a. detested
   b. parted
   c. hated

30. defiled
   a. polluted
   b. shattered
   c. stained

31. hoard
   a. dungeon
   b. store
   c. stockpile

32. coronet
   a. tiara
   b. cannon
   c. crown

33. amity
   a. goodwill
   b. awe
   c. friendship

34. conjunction
   a. hookup
   b. connection
   c. handle

35. discord
   a. sleeplessness
   b. clash
   c. disharmony

36. enmity
   a. silence
   b. hostility
   c. hatred

37. discourse
   a. conversation
   b. speech
   c. display

38. paramour
   a. sweetheart
   b. partner
   c. lover

39. apparel
   a. dress
   b. clothing
   c. shopping

40. pare
   a. trim
   b. slaughter
   c. prune

41. habitation
   a. foundation
   b. dwelling
   c. residence

42. transfigured
   a. transformed
   b. changed
   c. decayed

43. premeditated
   a. thought-out
   b. prearranged
   c. evil

44. throttle
   a. choke
   b. slap
   c. strangle

45. audacious
   a. foolish
   b. daring
   c. fearless

46. tarrying
   a. hiding
   b. waiting
   c. lingering

47. amend
   a. correct
   b. prepare
   c. repair

48. quell
   a. crush
   b. drink
   c. suppress

49. mote
   a. speck
   b. shower
   c. dot

50. reprehend
   a. blame
   b. scold
   c. discover

Improvisation: Student Enrichment

Research:

1. Prepare a report on the various stage productions of *A Midsummer Night's Dream.*

2. Write a paper on the musical adaptations of *A Midsummer Night's Dream.* Be sure to include a discussion of Felix Mendelssohn's famous adaptation.

3. Compare and contrast Shakespeare's use of comedic elements in *Twelfth Night* and in *A Midsummer Night's Dream.*

4. Make a list of mythical allusions from *A Midsummer Night's Dream.* Tell how five of these allusions relate to the plot, theme, or symbolism of the play.

5. Compare and contrast the use of the Pyramus and Thisby myth in *A Midsummer Night's Dream* and in *Romeo and Juliet.*

6. Is there a modern equivalent to Shakespeare's city/green world dichotomy? If you think there is, explain your contemporary version of the dichotomy. If you do not think there is a modern equivalent, explain why you think this dichotomy is no longer applicable.

Reaction:

1. Read aloud some of the passages which seem most significant to you. Explain how Shakespeare's choice of language adds to each passage.

2. The play includes many references to May, the moon, sleep, dreams, and other symbols linked with love. Which of these symbols are still meaningful today?

3. Why do you think Shakespeare included the fairies and Puck in the play? What do they add to the plot and theme?

Creation/Composition:

1. Do a modern adaptation of Act I, Scene 1. Update language, situations, and reactions.

2. Write a soliloquy giving Hermia's reaction to one of the alternatives given her by Theseus: (a) marry Demetrius; (b) take a vow to never marry; (c) be put to death.

3. Compose an ode to Bottom. Be sure to refer to his acting ability, his magical transformation, and his "love affair" with Titania.

4. Write a newspaper review of the performance of the play-within-a-play in *A Midsummer's Night Dream*. Be sure to include your nomination for best actor.

5. Draft the epilogue for the play-within-the-play that Bottom never delivers. Include morals or lessons in your epilogue that could apply both to Pyramus and Thisby's experiences and the experiences of the other lovers in the play.

6. Create a poster or a play bill for the Pyramus and Thisby play.

Between the Lines: Essay Test

Literal Level

1. According to Renaissance traditions, love often blossomed at first sight. However, love was said to be inconstant or changeable and was even likened to war. How are these traditions illustrated in *A Midsummer Night's Dream*?

2. What character parallels are there in *A Midsummer Night's Dream*?

3. What makes Bottom so amusing?

4. The Pyramus and Thisby myth is tragic. How has Shakespeare adapted it to a comic play?

Interpretive Level

1. How might Oberon in *A Midsummer Night's Dream* be compared to fate in other plays of Shakespeare?

2. Explain the "city world/green world" dichotomy in the play.

3. What is the symbolic significance of the Indian boy?

4. At what point does the action in *A Midsummer Night's Dream* climax?

Final Curtain: Objective Test

I. True—False

Mark each statement T for True or F for False.

________ 1. Egeus wants Hermia to marry Lysander.

________ 2. Theseus says that Hermia must either marry the man her father chooses or leave Athens.

________ 3. Helena loves Demetrius, though he has never returned her affection.

________ 4. Nick Bottom is a ham who boasts he can play any part.

________ 5. The original cause of Oberon and Titania's quarrel is Titania's jealousy of Hippolyta.

_______ 6. Puck uses magic to make Lysander fall in love with Helena.

_______ 7. Titania pretends to fall in love with Bottom to spite Oberon.

_______ 8. Bottom flees his friends in shame when he discovers he looks like an ass.

_______ 9. Helena believes Lysander and Demetrius are mocking her when they swear they love her.

_______ 10. Hermia reacts to Lysander's desertion of her by becoming angry at Helena.

_______ 11. Oberon is pleased and amused by the confusion that arises from Puck's mistake.

_______ 12. Titania is reconciled with Oberon after she gives him an Indian boy to be his attendant.

_______ 13. Theseus comes to the forest to find the runaway lovers.

_______ 14. Three pairs of mortal lovers marry by the end of the play.

_______ 15. The Pyramus and Thisby play turns out to be surprisingly sweet and touching.

II. Multiple Choice

Choose the best answer to complete each statement.

16. As duke of Athens, Theseus is

    a. brutal.
    b. indecisive.
    c. firm.

17. The duke plans a festival to celebrate

    a. his victory over the Amazons.
    b. his wedding.
    c. Midsummer Night's Eve.

18. Hermia's punishment for refusing to marry Demetrius is death or

    a. life imprisonment.
    b. torture.
    c. banishment to a nunnery.

19. Hermia and Lysander originally plan to take refuge with

    a. Lysander's father.
    b. Hermia's sister.
    c. Lysander's aunt.

20. Lysander and Hermia meet in the woods to

    a. find the king and queen of the fairies.
    b. say good-bye to each other before Hermia is married.
    c. sneak away to be married.

21. Demetrius learns about Hermia and Lysander's planned meeting from

    a. Helena.
    b. Egeus.
    c. Puck.

22. Puck is best known for his

    a. sweet, sensitive temper.
    b. love of practical jokes.
    c. devotion to Titania.

23. Titania is reluctant to give the Indian boy to Oberon because she

    a. wants to spite Oberon.
    b. loved the boy's mother.
    c. plans to give the boy to Theseus as a wedding gift.

24. As a result of Titania and Oberon's quarrel, the

    a. citizens of Athens are at war.
    b. duke has forbidden anyone to enter the woods.
    c. seasons have been disrupted.

25. Peaseblossom and Cobweb are

    a. citizens of Athens.
    b. members of Titania's fairy band.
    c. actors in Bottom's troupe.

26. The comedy of errors begins when Puck mistakenly puts a spell on

    a. Helena.
    b. Lysander.
    c. Demetrius.

27. Bottom and his fellow actors are worried that their play might be too

    a. scholarly and dry.
    b. frightening and sad.
    c. comical and ridiculous.

28. Many of the transformations in the play take place when the characters are

    a. frightened.
    b. asleep.
    c. drunk.

29. Bottom and his friends are best described as

    a. a professional acting troupe.
    b. unsophisticated craftsmen.
    c. comical court nobles.

30. Bottom thinks his friends flee him in the woods because they

a. want to scare him.
b. don't recognize him.
c. are frightened of fairies.

31. The philosophy is often expressed in the play that

a. love is blind.
b. romantic love brings peace and harmony.
c. passion often produces tragedy.

32. Puck keeps Lysander and Demetrius from fighting by

a. tripping them and stealing their swords.
b. imitating their voices and putting them to sleep.
c. pretending to be Helena and calling for help.

33. In the end, Demetrius finally loves

a. Hippolyta.
b. Hermia.
c. Helena.

34. The play-within-the-play is

a. a dramatic highlight.
b. comic relief.
c. a lyrical interlude.

35. At the end of the play, the lovers are all blessed by

a. Theseus.
b. Egeus.
c. the fairies.

III. Matching

A. Match each character with the proper description.

______	36. Bottom	a. Amazon queen; Theseus' bride
______	37. Titania	b. Oberon's mischievous sprite
______	38. Theseus	c. maid who loves Lysander
______	39. Puck	d. blonde who betrays her friend
______	40. Hermia	e. queen of the fairies
______	41. Lysander	f. under Puck's spell, he rejects Hermia
______	42. Oberon	g. king of the fairies
______	43. Hippolyta	h. weaver given an ass's head
______	44. Demetrius	i. Hermia's unwelcome suitor
______	45. Helena	j. duke of Athens

B. Match each item with the proper description.

______ 46. Theseus' palace
______ 47. love-in-idleness
______ 48. malapropism
______ 49. woods outside Athens
______ 50. duke's edict

a. where magic rules
b. word comically misused
c. where order reigns
d. bars Hermia from marrying her true love
e. magic flower